101 killer apps

for your Palm™ Handheld

About the Authors

Dave Johnson is a technology journalist with nearly three dozen books to his credit. He writes *PC World*'s Digital Focus (a weekly digital photography newsletter) and is the former editor of *Mobility Magazine.* He's an award-winning wildlife photographer and the author of *The Wild Cookie,* an interactive children's story on CD-ROM. Dave is also a dedicated—but entirely talentless—guitarist, though he tries to make up for that deficiency by dressing like Pink Floyd's Roger Waters. Before Dave started writing, his somewhat unfocused career included flying satellites, driving an ice cream truck, photographing a rock band, stocking shelves at Quick Check, teaching rocket science, and writing novels about intergalactic space penguins. Today, he relaxes by photographing wolves; he's also a SCUBA instructor and underwater photographer.

Rick Broida has been a technology writer for nearly 15 years. He is the founder and former editor of *Handheld Computing Magazine* and the author of over a dozen books, including the best-selling *How to Do Everything with Your Palm Handheld* (McGraw-Hill/Osborne, 2003). Broida's writing credits include Cnet, *Computer Shopper, PC Magazine,* and *Wired.* He lives in Michigan with his wife and two children, where he authors the Tech Savvy column for Michigan's *Observer & Eccentric* newspapers. His hobbies include basketball, kickboxing, and computer gaming.

Denny Atkin has been writing about technology since 1987 and about handheld computers since the Newton's release in 1993. He's worked with pioneering technology magazines as such as *Compute!, Omni,* and *Handheld Computing.* Atkin lives with his wife and son in Vermont, a state where PDAs are nearly as popular as maple syrup.

101 killer apps

for your Palm™ Handheld

Dave Johnson and **Rick Broida**

McGraw-Hill/Osborne

New York Chicago San Francisco Lisbon
London Madrid Mexico City Milan New Delhi
San Juan Seoul Singapore Sydney Toronto

The McGraw-Hill Companies

McGraw-Hill/Osborne
2100 Powell Street, 10th Floor
Emeryville, California 94608
U.S.A.

To arrange bulk purchase discounts for sales promotions, premiums, or fund-raisers, please contact **McGraw-Hill/**Osborne at the above address. For information on translations or book distributors outside the U.S.A., please see the International Contact Information page immediately following the index of this book.

101 Killer Apps for Your Palm™ Handheld

1234567890 FGR FGR 01987654

Book p/n 0-07-225430-0 and CD p/n 0-07-225431-9
parts of
ISBN 0-07-225429-7

Publisher	Brandon A. Nordin
Vice President and Associate Publisher	Scott Rogers
Executive Editor	Jane K. Brownlow
Project Editor	Emily K. Wolman
Project Manager	LeeAnn Pickrell
Acquisitions Coordinator	Agatha Kim
Technical Editor	Denny Atkin
Copy Editor	Bill McManus
Proofreader	Susie Elkind
Indexer	Karin Arrigoni
Composition	Kelly Stanton-Scott
Illustrators	Melinda Lytle, Kathleen Edwards
Series Design	Kelly Stanton-Scott, Peter F. Hancik

This book was composed with Corel VENTURA™ Publisher.

Dave dedicates this book to Killer Application number 102, which,
though it tried hard and seemed to have all the right moves, just
missed appearing in this book by the slimmest of margins.
We mourn for you, sweet, innocent Killer App 102.

Why, oh why, was this book limited to just 101 killer apps?
Mercy hath taken her leave of us!
–Dave

For Shawna, who gave me two beautiful children.
–Rick

Contents at a Glance

Contents

Acknowledgments

What more can be said about the superb folks at Osborne McGraw-Hill? Without Jane Brownlow, Agatha Kim, and Emily Wolman, this book would be little more than incoherent notes on a napkin. Kind thanks also to Bill McManus, Susie Elkind, and Valerie Perry. The OMH staff is, after all these many books, more than editors—they're friends, confidants, and, as is often the case, bail bonds. We also want to thank our good friend Denny Atkin, who, though he was raised by dingoes in the Australian Outback, nonetheless keeps flagging our libelously inaccurate comments.

Dave adds:

You can't spend a few months of your life writing a book without a great support system of friends and family. Thanks to my great kids, Evan and Marin. They may not realize it, but their insistence that I'm funny keeps me writing. Thanks to my wife, Kristen, for her constant help. And thanks to Rick for being such a great friend, patient colleague, and talented coauthor. I have just five words for you, buddy: "You're making me look bad."

Rick adds:

Right back at ya, pal. My heartfelt thanks go out not only to Dave, whose grammatically questionable prose and unique brand of "humor" make my writing look much better, but also to Shawna, Sarah, and Ethan, who have to put up with the inevitable grumpiness that comes from having too much work and too little time. Thanks for all the pop runs and "vacation Tuesdays."

Introduction

We make no secret of our love of PDAs. They're such amazing little devices, packing more computing power than many desktop systems of yesteryear. Indeed, while most people purchase PDAs primarily for their organizational capabilities, they can do much more—much, much more. Much.

It was with that in mind that we wrote this book. It's time for you to learn just how capable your PDA really is, from helping you count calories to showing you last night's episode of *Alias*. This book is all about using your Palm OS PDA to do unexpected, unusual, and fun stuff. We've rounded up 101 of the best programs available for the Palm OS and offered them up for you on a silver platter. Literally. The silver platter (otherwise known as a CD-ROM) at the back of this book is crammed with most of the programs we discuss in this book. That means you can read about a program and install it immediately—no need to locate it on the Internet and then download it (though this is the case for a few).

By the way, you might be wondering what we mean when say "Palm OS PDA." Are we talking only about PalmOne (formerly Palm, Inc.) devices like the Zire 71 and Tungsten T3? Not by a long shot. This book is for anyone who has a device that runs the Palm operating system. That includes not only PalmOne-branded models, but also those from companies like Sony, Samsung, Handspring, and Garmin. No matter what kind of Palm device you have, this book's killer apps will help you do more and have more fun.

What's Inside

This book is arranged into 10 chapters, each one dedicated to a different way to use your PDA. We start you off with a bunch of great tools for getting more out of your PDA at work—Chapter 1 is filled with killer apps that help you deliver PowerPoint presentations from a PDA, manage your phone calls, carry databases on your PDA, and even read Adobe Acrobat (PDF) documents. From there, we look at applications designed to make your next trip more fun and productive with city guide software, restaurant guides, language translators, and more. And that's the way the book works. In subsequent chapters, we offer diversions like e-books, wine selection, exercise, and digital music. There are chapters full of games, money managers, utilities to make your Palm run better, and more. If it's a killer app, you can read about in the book, then install it from the bundled CD.

Killer Tip *In most cases, what you'll find on the CD are trial versions of software. If you like a program and want to keep using it past its trial period, then you need to pay a small shareware registration fee to get unlimited access to the full program.*

We'd also like to draw your attention to a few special elements that we included to help you get the most out of the book:

- **Notes** These paragraphs include interesting stuff that will help you win the next edition of *Trivial Pursuit: Obscure Facts About Books Written by Dave and Rick Edition.*
- **Killer Tips** These miraculous tidbits of prose tell you how to do something smarter or faster.
- **Sidebars** In each chapter, you'll find a tip so great, so helpful, and so amazing that we decided to put it in its own special box.
- **Find It on the CD** At the end of each killer application, we give you all the cold, hard stats about the program—what the full, commercial version costs, the name of the developer, and where to find it on the Web. This is what the box looks like:

FIND IT ON THE CD
Wine Enthusiast Guide, $19.95
LandWare
www.landware.com

Installing Software on Your PDA

So, you want to be a rock star? Well, then you're reading the wrong book. But if you're ready to dig into this tome and explore all the cool programs we have to offer you, then you might want to know how to install all those apps on your device.

You can install almost any app in this book in either of two ways:

- Grab the program from the bundled CD-ROM. The CD is organized by number, just like the programs in this book. Thus, to find a specific program, just find its number and follow the supplied links to install it on your PC or find it on the Web.

- Find it on and download it from the Internet using the URL that we provide in the box at the end of each application description.

Which is better? It depends. The CD is faster, which is why we gave it to you to begin with. But in some cases, there might be a better, newer version of the program on the Internet, so the Web is a pretty good route as well. It's up to you.

Here's the secret to installing apps on your PDA: the mnemonic DUI. DUI stands for download, unzip, install. The first part is easy: go to the appropriate web site (like www.palmgear.com, for instance) or look on the CD, find the app that you want, and then download or copy the Zip file that represents the program onto your desktop. That's the *download* part.

Killer Tip *Make sure you take note of where you're saving the downloaded file! We recommend just putting it on the Windows desktop (or in your My Documents folder), as it'll be easy to find. You can simply delete it after installing the program on the PDA.*

Now for the *unzip* part. Most programs distributed online—especially those that consist of multiple files—are compressed and collected into a single file using the popular Zip format. That means you need a way to open—or "unzip"—the file; you can't just install the Zip on your handheld. If you're a Windows XP user, you're all set: that version of Windows can access Zip files directly. Just double-click the zipped file. A window will open containing a list of one or more files. At least one file will end with .prc; others may have a .pdb extension. And there may be other files with endings like .txt, .doc, or .htm.

Here's what you need to know: the PRC and PDB files get installed on the PDA; any other files are simply there to help you get through the install. So if the Zip contains only a PRC file, for instance, just install it. But if there's a readme file (usually called readme.txt or readme.htm), open it and follow its directions.

Note *If you're not a Windows XP user, you'll need WinZip—a shareware program you must download and install prior to trying to install any Palm OS applications. You can get it from www.winzip.com. Once it's installed, you can double-click any Zip files and get the same results as we explained above.*

Note *Some programs have their own installers (usually a single file called setup.exe), meaning you needn't monkey around with Zip or PRC files. Just double-click the installer and follow the directions.*

Finally, you're ready for the *install* step, where you arrange for the app to be copied to your handheld the next time you HotSync. This couldn't be easier: just double-click the PRC file. You'll then see the program appear in the PDA's Install Tool dialog box. If you have any other files—like a second PRC or a few PDB files—to install, you can drag and drop them into this same dialog box. Then just HotSync, and you're done!

Now go forth and enjoy the book!

Stay in Touch

Can't get enough of Dave or Rick? You can send any questions and comments to dave@bydavejohnson.com or rickbroida1@excite.com. Thanks, and enjoy reading the book!

Chapter 1

On the Job

Ah, work. Is any task so sweet, any labor so gratifying? Dost anything but the fresh feeling of driving into the office inspire such poetry in our hearts?

Well, probably. Right off the top of our heads, we can think of a dozen things we'd rather do than work. On the other hand, throw your Palm into the work mix and you have something else entirely. Palm PDAs can lighten your workload and make it easier to get jobs done on the go. Most of all, using your PDA to work is just plain cool. Instead of hauling out a seven-pound laptop, imagine slipping a five-ounce Palm out of your pocket—and getting essentially the same work done. In this chapter, we've found a slew of ways for you to work more efficiently by employing a PDA instead of a desktop PC, laptop, tablet, or some other nineteenth-century contraption. Dig in, and have a better day at work!

1 Presenter-to-Go

Biz Presentations: From Palm to Projector

POWER APP

You're on the road, many miles from home. What's it take to deliver a PowerPoint presentation in someone else's conference room? If you were lucky, the old answer was "a laptop to connect to the LCD projector already in the room." Worst case, you'd have to haul not just the laptop, but a portable projector as well. Talk about sore shoulders.

These days, you can leave the laptop at home. There are a couple of products available that connect your Palm directly to a projector, cutting out the laptop middleman. That's right—your pocket-sized PDA is more than powerful enough to display full-resolution PowerPoint slides on an LCD projector. The bottom line is that they look just as good as if you used a laptop.

What magical products do this sort of thing? Our favorite is a gadget called Presenter-to-Go from MARGI Systems. There are several versions of Presenter-to-Go available, but for most Palm PDAs, look for the SD Card version. A small SD Card adapter slips into the SD Card slot of your Palm and connects directly to the VGA port of an LCD projector (see Figure 1-1). You then control the PowerPoint slides either by using buttons on the Palm or, if you'd rather walk around the room and put some distance between yourself and the projector, by using the small credit card–sized remote that comes with it.

Killer Tip *If you have ever said, "I wish there was an easy way to display a Palm's screen on a big screen so lots of people can see at once," you're in luck. Presenter-to-Go comes with a utility called MARGI Mirror. This program duplicates the Palm's screen and shows it, more or less in real time, on the projector. You can use it to perform PDA training classes, for instance, demonstrating techniques on the Palm screen as the display responds to your every screen tap.*

There are two ways to get the slides into your Palm. Using the software that comes with Presenter-to-Go, you can simply open your slideshow in PowerPoint, then save the file as a Palm-ready file and HotSync to transfer it to your PDA. If you also have

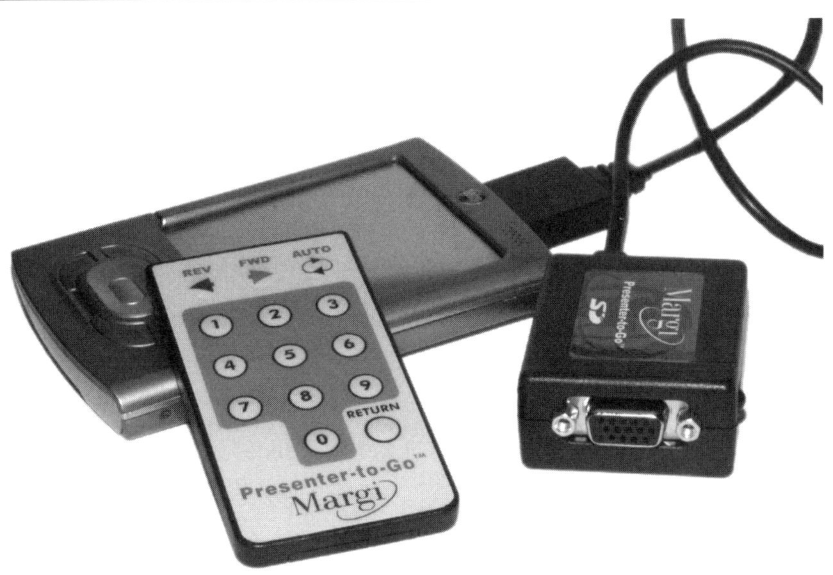

FIGURE 1-1 Presenter-to-Go attaches to your PDA and displays PowerPoint slides on a traditional LCD projector.

DataViz Documents To Go (see Trick 9 at the end of this chapter), you can display true, unconverted PowerPoint slides with Presenter-to-Go directly—and even edit them on the PDA right up to the moment you need to display them. Consider these scenarios:

- You forgot to bring the slides with you. A quick call back to the office, and someone can e-mail the PowerPoint slides to you. Using an e-mail program and a wireless Palm, you can receive the slides, open them in Documents To Go, and deliver them on the big screen with Presenter-to-Go.
- You copied the PowerPoint slides to an SD Card at your desktop, popped the card into your PDA, and viewed the slides on your Palm. You notice a typo. Just open the slides in Documents To Go, make the changes (see Figure 1-2), and immediately deliver the presentation using Presenter-to-Go.

And you did it all without a laptop.

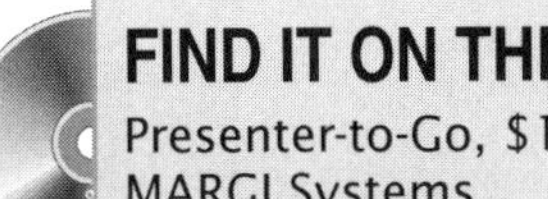

FIND IT ON THE CD

Presenter-to-Go, $199
MARGI Systems
www.margi.com

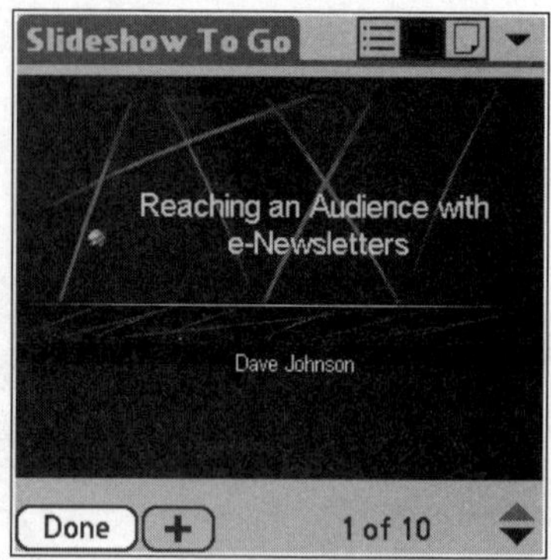

FIGURE 1-2 Documents To Go and Presenter-to-Go work well together for editing, displaying, and projecting PowerPoint slides.

2 ThoughtManager

Outline Your Thoughts and Ideas

Everyone has a little genius hidden away in them. At least, that's what Rick's mom told him when he accidentally put his pants on backwards. Last week. Nonetheless, getting your spark of brilliance out of your head and onto paper, into PowerPoint, or in whatever vehicle will get you promoted to company VP sometimes takes a little coaxing. The Palm Memo Pad may be fine for writing down your ideas in a linear way, but it's weak when it comes to rearranging and fine-tuning those ideas. Instead, try an idea organizer.

ThoughtManager, from Hands High Software, is an ideal way to articulate and polish ideas, projects, outlines, and other day-to-day documents. ThoughtManager is an outliner—it lets you "nest" your ideas into a structure that represents the way the data in your head is actually related and connected. Imagine you're outlining a tip report. You might make these notes in your Palm:

Exec Meeting

- Vision statement
- Approved upgrades

Factory Tour

- Can we get a pool table like theirs?
- Innovative security
- Eye scanners
- Passive card readers

Once you are back on your desktop, you can obviously hone these notes into a complete report. But it's obviously easier with an organized outline that you've been able to complete on your PDA. Here's how to do it with ThoughtManager:

1. Start the program and tap New. This begins a new project.
2. Enter a name for this outline in the space that currently says Untitled.
3. To make your first entry, tap the star at the bottom of the screen. Then enter information on this new line.

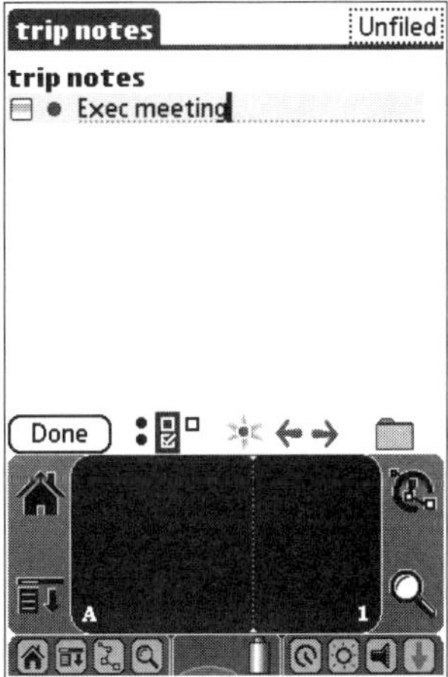

4. If you want to "nest" or indent information under this main heading, tap the star again to make a new entry, then tap the right arrow icon to indent. You can add any number of nested statements by tapping the star.
5. When you're ready to create a new main heading, tap the star and then tap the left arrow to "promote" this entry to the first level. It's that easy!

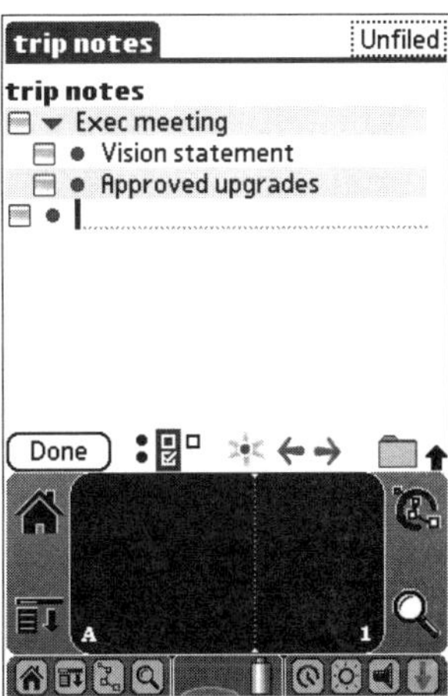

Killer Tip *If you want to add data to your outline but you're not sure where it fits, store it in the folder for later. Just drag your text by the bullet or arrow and drop it in the folder at the bottom of the screen. The folder can hold any number of bullets, and you can pull them out of the folder and insert them in the outline anytime you like.*

FIND IT ON THE CD
ThoughtManager, $39.95
Hands High Software
www.handshigh.com

3 TAKEphONE

Manage Your Phone Calls

If you've got a Palm OS device that doubles as a phone—like the Treo 600, for instance—or one that connects to your phone via Bluetooth or infrared, then you've probably struggled with a seemingly simple problem. How do you easily dial numbers in the Palm Address Book?

The Palm OS itself makes it somewhat simple. Just switch to your list of contacts and tap on the entry for someone you want to call. Depending upon which PDA or Palm smartphone you own, you'll then just tap the phone number or a "Quick Connect" icon to dial the number.

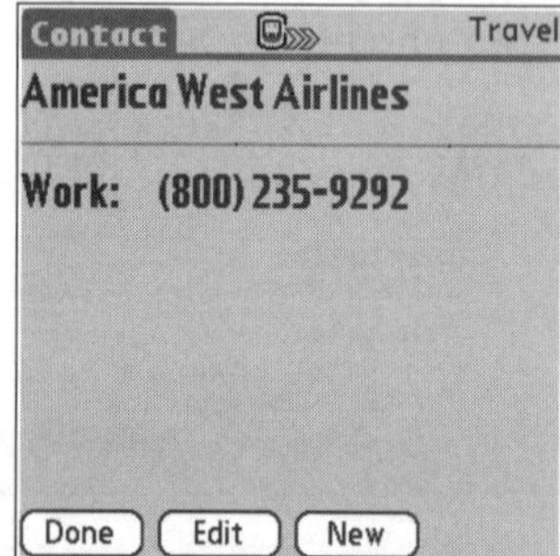

But that's a lot of steps, and one of the trickiest jobs is just finding the right phone number to begin with. There's a better way.

Install a program called TAKEphONE. Though it's strangely named, this program lets you manage and organize your phone activities in a very powerful way. Here's what the program looks like:

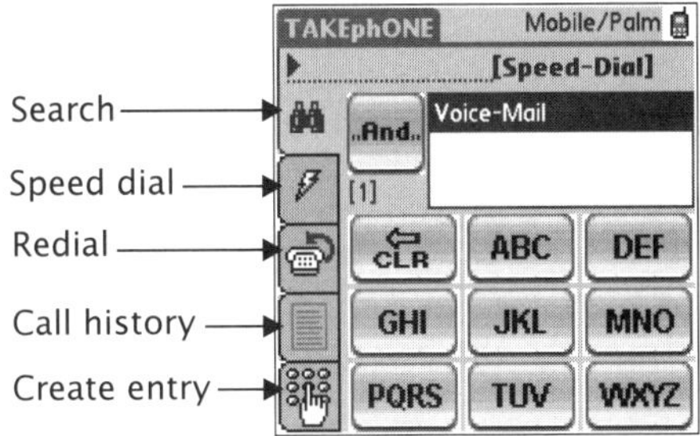

Here's where the program shows its worth. With the first tab (the Search tab) selected, tap out the name of someone you want to find. See the And button? That means you can do a Boolean search for someone. What's that mean? Suppose you want to quickly find an entry for Dave Johnson from an address list that has thousands of entries:

1. Tap DEF, then ABC, then TUV. TAKEphONE lists every name in the list that uses any of those letters, like DAV, EAT, or FAT.

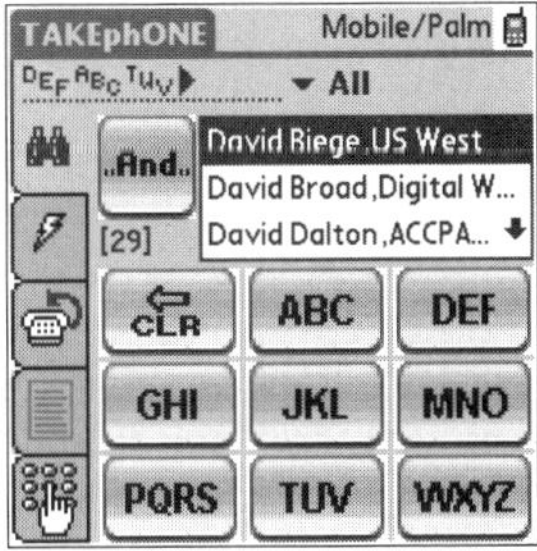

2. Tap the And button.
3. Now enter part of the last name. To enter JOH, tap JKL, MNO, and GHI.
4. In all likelihood, TAKEphONE will narrow the search down to just the one entry you are looking for. Tap it.
5. Tap the number to dial your phone.

Killer Tip *To clear a search, tap and hold the CLR button for several seconds.*

TAKEphONE has many other features, including the ability to redial numbers and add common numbers to the speed-dial list. It's an essential tool for any PDA that has the ability to place phone calls.

FIND IT ON THE CD

TAKEphONE, $19.95
ShSh
www.shsh.com

4 MegaCalc

Perform Complex Calculations

Looking for a better calculator? No, it's not quite as exciting as a better music player, a better car, or a better mousetrap. But the calculator that comes with your PDA is pretty anemic—it adds, subtracts, multiplies, and divides. (If you didn't know there was a calculator in your PDA, just look for a program called Calc in the Application screen, with the category set to All).

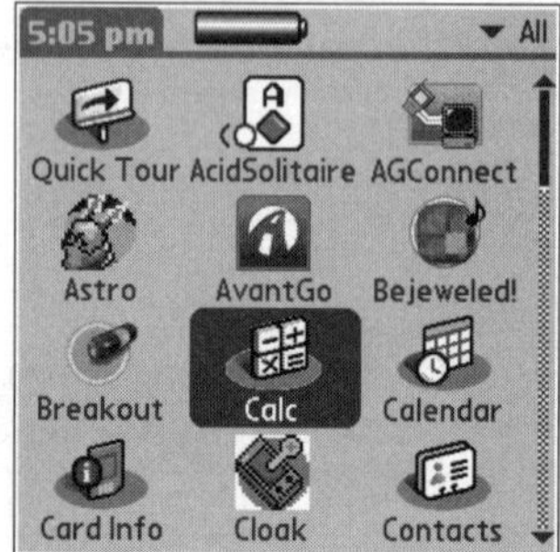

If you want to do more, you need to add a new calculator to your device.

MegaCalc, from MegaSoft2000, has a variety of operating modes that are easily accessed from the Mode menu. You can use the Simple Mode, which behaves like a traditional four-function calculator, or try the Engineering Mode, which offers up SIN, COS, TAN, LOG, and many other features. The calculator will also do conversion between bases, such as decimal, hex, and binary.

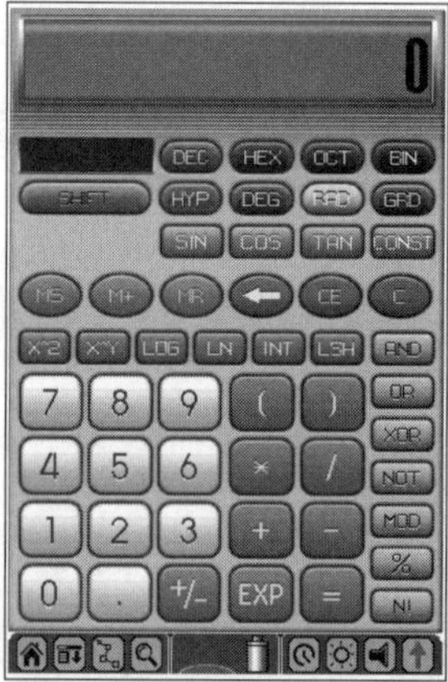

Unit conversions are a great way to convert, say, pounds to kilograms. There are many conversions available—to do a unit conversion, just choose Unit Conversion from the menu and choose the type of unit you want to work with. Then pick a From and a

To, and enter the number you want to covert. In this way, you can find that there are 33.02 feet of seawater in each atmosphere of pressure.

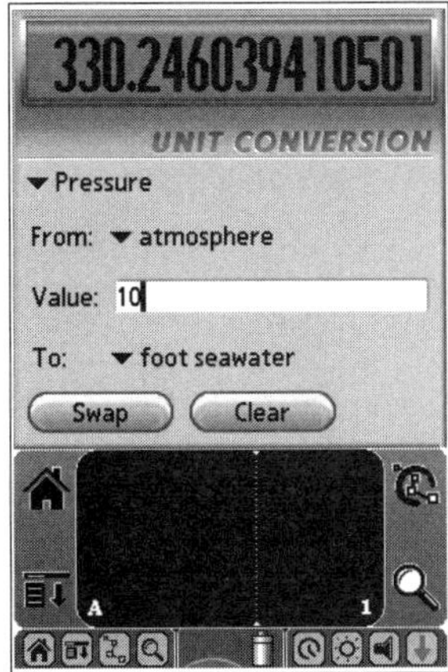

That's not all: there's also a currency calculator, tip calculator, and even a mortgage engine in MegaCalc. It's an all-in-one math problem solver.

FIND IT ON THE CD
MegaCalc, $14.95
MegaSoft2000
www.megasoft2000.com

5 Quickoffice

Word Processing Power for Palms

Until recently, claiming that you wanted to get a PDA to do some word processing on the go was little more than a joke. Palm's Memo Pad, for instance, limits you to an anemic 4,000 characters, which is about 500 words or a page of text. There's no spell check, formatting, or other fancy features. The best you can hope for with Memo Pad, in fact, is simply to write something on the go and then later edit it massively once you are back on the desktop.

Not anymore. There are a handful of word processors available for the Palm OS that make working on the road almost as comfortable as working at your desk. Quickoffice, from iGo, for instance, delivers powerful Word and Excel compatibility for just $40.

Want to type a document in Quickoffice? You can use Graffiti or the tiny Chiclet-style keyboard that's built into some PDAs, but we suggest getting an accessory keyboard. Something like the Palm Wireless Keyboard gives you full-size, laptop-like typing. Once you've got your keyboard and a copy of Quickoffice in hand, you're ready to type. On the main screen, tap the New document button, then just start typing.

Killer Tip *You can convert a Quickoffice document into an e-book that's readable on almost any PDA. It's a handy way to share portable documents.*

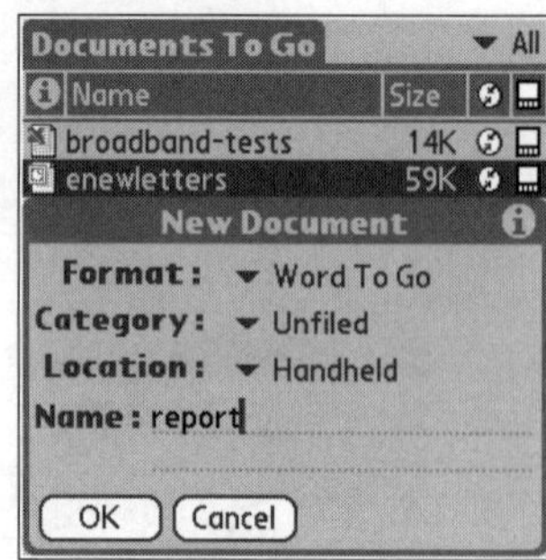

Notice that you have the ability to change the font style, size, and attributes by tapping the icons at the bottom of the screen. You also have access to paragraph formatting and a Search & Replace icon.

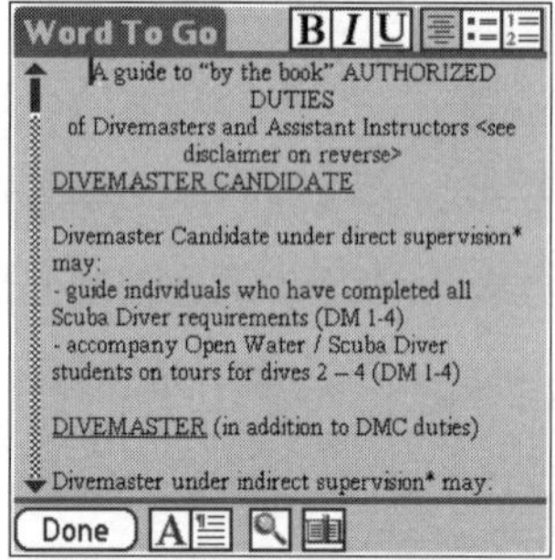

The menus are full of additional word-processing controls as well. The Options menu, for instance, holds a thesaurus, spell check, and even the ability to use multiple dictionaries.

Good news: when you HotSync your PDA, the document you created will appear on your PC in Word format. That means you can load your mobile documents into Word and finish them up in a format that anyone with a computer can read and use.

FIND IT ON THE CD
Quickoffice, $39.95
iGo
www.quickoffice.com

Databases to Go

Your PDA is a great place to keep track of data—personal information, customer or client data, field research, you name it. If you've ever thought that your Palm was a smart place to track information but you didn't want to use a free-form text file like the Memo Pad, then a database application might be right for you.

Handmark's MobileDB is a great database application to get your feet wet in mobile databases. Using MobileDB, you can create your own databases, reference databases that have been made elsewhere in your company, download new ones from the Web, and more. How to get started? Easy. After you install MobileDB, just follow these steps to create your own database:

1. When you start MobileDB, you see a list of all the database files stored on your Palm. You can tap any one of them to open and review the data.

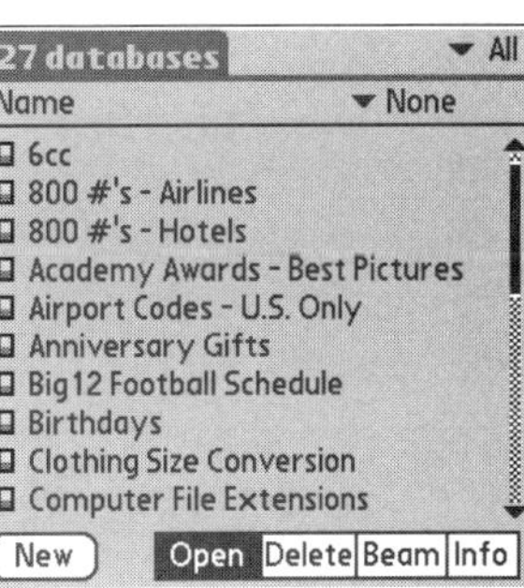

2. To create a new database from scratch, tap New.
3. In the Create Database dialog box, enter a name. Suppose we're going to make a database to collect information about customer satisfaction as we travel from client to client. Name this database Client Satisfaction and click OK.
4. There will be three fields in this database. The first field will be the client's name. The second field will store the kind of equipment that is installed. The third field will be a record of the customer satisfaction on a scale of one to ten. On the Field Definitions screen, enter Client in the space for Field 1.
5. In Field 2, enter **Equipment**.
6. Finally, for Field 3, enter **Satisfaction** and change the type of field from Text to Number. Tap Done.

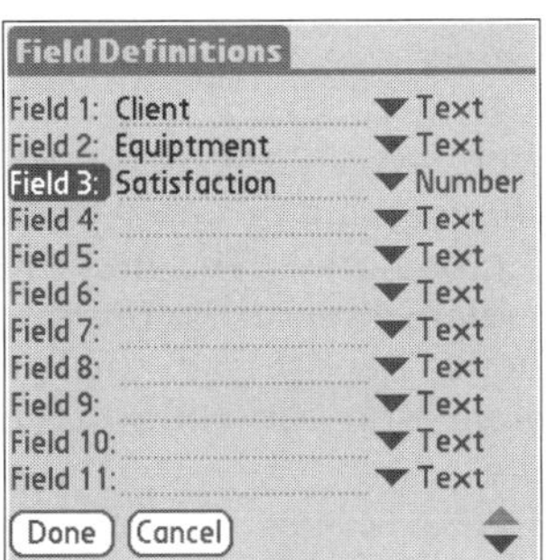

7. You are now taken to the database itself. You can enter data by tapping the New button and tapping Done when the data is complete. Here you can see a completed database with information stored within:

Client Satisfaction

Client	Equiptment	Satisfacti
Stevens	13A1	5
Johnson	2317	7
Jones	14A1	8

Done New 1 of 3

FIND IT ON THE CD
MobileDB, $19.95
Handmark
www.handmark.com

7 ExpensePlus

Can You Expense an Expense Tracker?

Business trips can be costly. Sure, the boss is supposed to pick up the tab. But that doesn't always happen, mostly because you forget to file your expenses. In other words, stop griping: it's your own fault.

Thankfully, there's an easy way to solve this problem. By installing an expense tracker on your PDA, you can stay on top of all your expenses as they happen and pour them all into an expense spreadsheet on the PC when you return. There's more than one way to do this. Many Palm OS devices, for instance, come with an expense program built right into the operating system.

But not all do. And even if yours does, you may not like that simple utility anyway. Instead, we suggest that you install a program called ExpensePlus from WalletWare.

Using ExpensePlus is pretty simple. The first time you start the program, you'll be asked to create a new expense report (in the future, you can create new reports by choosing File | New Expense Report from the Palm's menu).

Give the report a name and enter any information you like on that screen, then click Save.

From here, you should see a screen with lots of colorful icons for the many sorts of business expenses you might encounter on your trip. To add a lunch expense to your report, for instance, tap the menu under the first icon (it has plates and silverware) and choose Lunch.

On the Expense Slip, fill in all the details, such as the amount of the meal, how you paid for it, and the description.

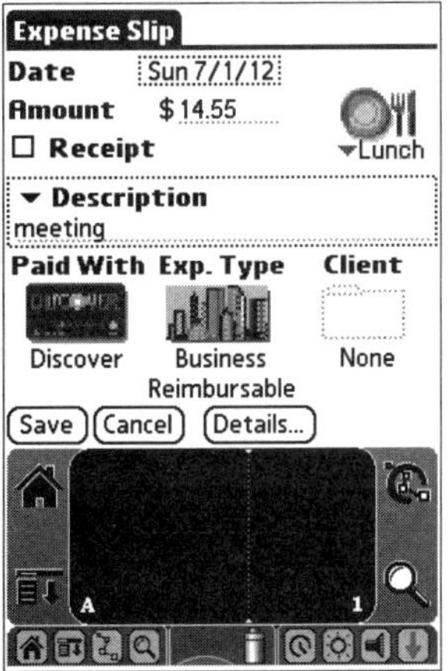

At the bottom of the slip, be sure to select all three pieces of info by clicking on the icons:

- How did you pay? You can select credit cards, cash, or check.
- What is the reimbursement category? You can specify business or personal.
- Was a client involved? You can associate the item with a specific client for tracking purposes.

When you're done, click Save to add this slip to your travel expense report.

You can continue to add expenses to your report until the trip is complete. When you return home, perform a HotSync. ExpensePlus automatically pours your business expense data (but not any personal expense entries) into an Excel spreadsheet that you can edit, save, or print.

FIND IT ON THE CD
ExpensePlus, $49.95
WalletWare
www.walletware.com

Put a PDF in Your Pocket

Even if you have a program like Documents To Go for carrying Word and Excel files in your PDA, there are still certain kinds of documents that just don't fit in a PDA. At least, you might not think that they do. Consider the good old PDF file. Also called Adobe Acrobat files, these documents are the mainstay of any office. PDFs get traded around like some sort of high tech, businessy baseball cards, and everyone is expected to be able to read them. That's great if you're in the office, but what if you are on the go? Can you copy a PDF file to your PDA and read it on the train, in a plane, or sunbathing on the yacht?

Sure you can. Get RepliGo from Cerience. RepliGo is a powerful document converter that lets you convert virtually any document—Word, Excel, PDF, web pages, PowerPoint, even Microsoft Project files—into a form that can be viewed on the PDA. In the process, nothing is lost. Indeed, on the Palm, documents look virtually identical to their desktop cousins. You can zoom in for a better view or zoom out and take in all (or most) of the document at once.

Here's how to create and view a PDF file on the Palm after installing RepliGo on your PDA:

1. Open a PDF file on your desktop computer.
2. Choose File | Print to see the Print dialog box.
3. From the list of available printers, choose RepliGo.

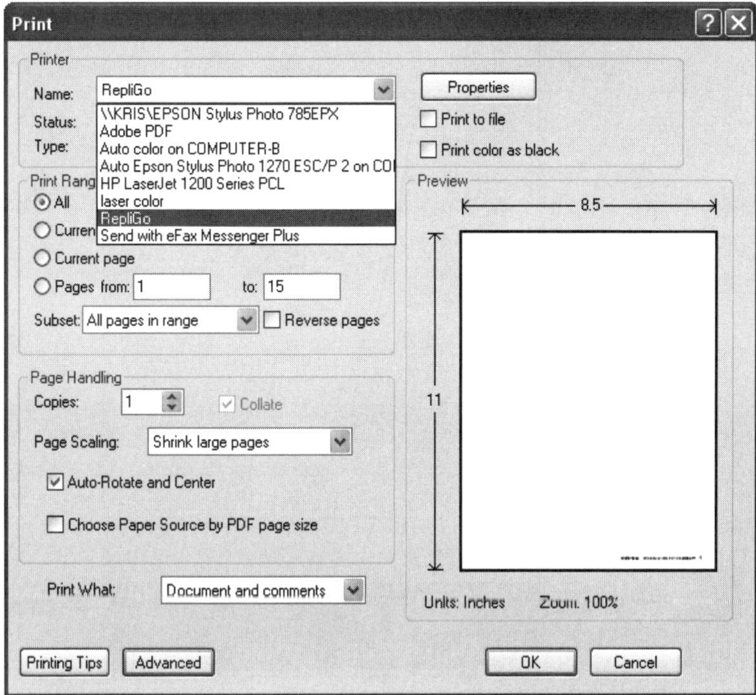

4. Specify the print range. If you want to convert the entire document to a RepliGo file and view it on the PDA, click OK. Otherwise, select just the page or pages you want to transfer.

5. After the "printing" process, you'll see a Convert Document dialog box. You can change the document's name (as it appears on the Palm), specify the location—handheld or memory card—and then click OK.

6. After the conversion, perform a HotSync.

7. Open RepliGo and choose the file from the list. Now you can use the controls at the bottom of the screen to read and navigate the document.

Killer Tip *Another way to get PDF files on your PC is by installing Acrobat Reader for Palm, available from www.adobe.com. It doesn't display any images, but it's free!*

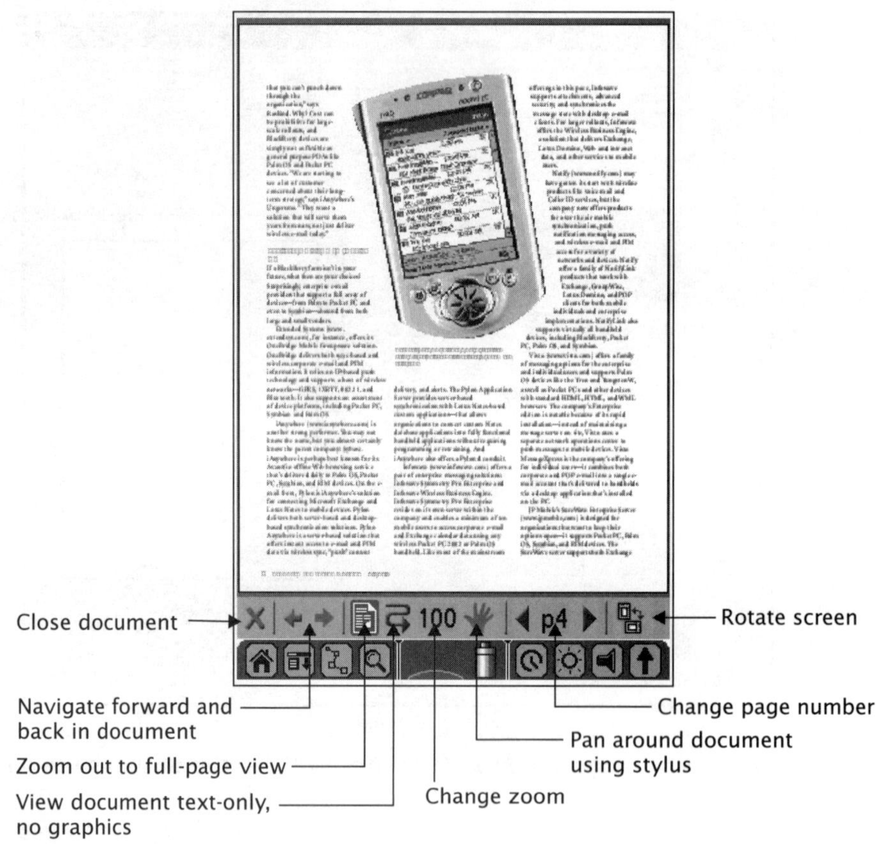

FIND IT ON THE CD
RepliGo, $29.95
Cerience
www.cerience.com

9 Documents To Go

Microsoft Office Goes Native

What a pain. Getting a Word or Excel document onto the Palm can be a frustrating experience. In order to edit a Word file from your desktop PC, for instance, you need an office productivity application like Quickword or Documents To Go. You need to drag the word file onto a desktop converter and then HotSync. Where's the spontaneity?

It's right here. The reality is that while that was the way you used to need to covert documents for your Palm, the newest versions of programs like Quickword and Documents To Go now support Word and Excel files in the native format, with no conversion needed at all.

Here's what that means: armed with Documents To Do 6 on your PDA, just follow these steps:

1. Grab the SD Card or Memory Stick from your PDA and insert it in your desktop PC's memory card reader.

2. Drag and drop any Word file onto the card.
3. Take the card out of the card reader and insert it into your Palm.
4. Start Documents To Go.
5. At the bottom of the screen, make sure the Show menu is set to Microsoft Word.

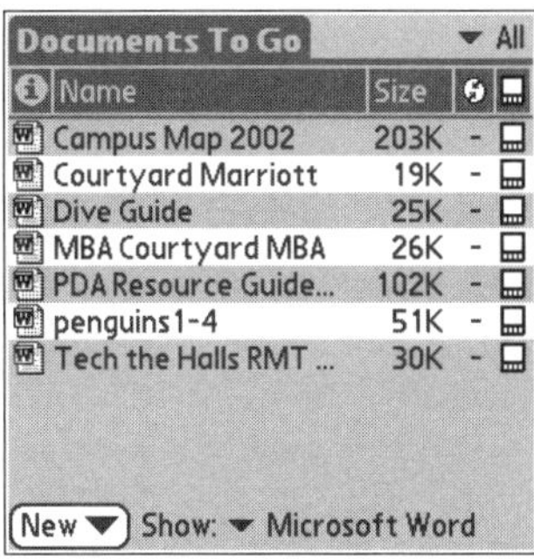

6. Tap the file to open it for editing or reference.

That's all there is to it. Of course, you might be saying: "Well, that's cool, but it's not a lot easier than just doing the old-fashioned conversion process. Is there more?"

There sure is. Since Documents To Go can read true Word and Excel files without conversion, you can get these files any way you like. You can "beam" them from another PDA using the IR port. You can get the files in e-mail if you use a program like SnapperMail or VersaMail that can retrieve attachments. You can receive files sent via Bluetooth. It opens up a lot of possibilities. Indeed—since Documents To Go can read and save files in Microsoft's own format, you can receive a Word document, edit it, and then use an e-mail program like SnapperMail to send it to someone's desktop PC. They'll never even know that your computer was a PDA.

FIND IT ON THE CD

Documents To Go, $29.95
DataViz
www.dataviz.com

Chapter 2

Bon Voyage!

As far as Rick is concerned, the only thing better than traveling is traveling light. Palm OS PDAs are ideal in that regard, as they enable you to carry books for reading, music for listening, movies for watching—and all the important items you need when taking a trip. We're talking reservation information, language dictionaries, street maps, even guides to local restaurants and hot spots. Why stuff all that stuff in your carry-on bag when you can pack it in your PDA instead?

10 Vindigo

Concierge in Your Pocket

POWER APP

Vindigo is the ultimate travel accessory. It provides up-to-the-minute dining, shopping, entertainment, and other leisure information for over 50 major U.S. cities (see the Vindigo web site for a complete list) and London. With just a tap or two, you can find restaurants and reviews, ATMs, bookstores, bars, clubs, flower shops, maps, movie theaters and show times, and plenty more. It even provides local weather and step-by-step walking directions from your current location to any other location in its database.

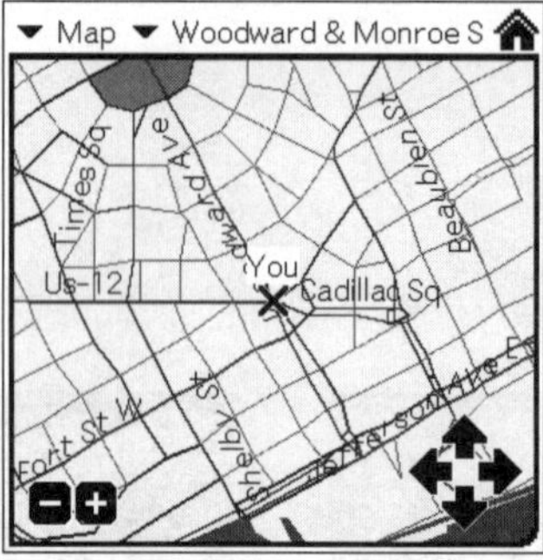

The service isn't free, but it's definitely affordable. You can pay a $3.50 monthly fee or subscribe for an entire year for $24.95.

Killer Tip *As with many Palm OS programs, you can try Vindigo before plunking down your hard-earned moola. The service offers a free 30-day trial version, which should give you ample opportunity to evaluate it. We think if you travel a lot or live in a big city, Vindigo is well worth the price of admission.*

So how does all this information get from Vindigo to your PDA? After you perform the initial installation of the software and set up your account, you use a web-based interface (see Figure 2-1) to choose which city (or cities) you want to include. Within each city, you can add or remove content channels—subsets of information, such as food, shops, movies, and services. (Each channel consumes some of your PDA's memory, so if there's information you don't necessarily need, it's best to deselect it.)

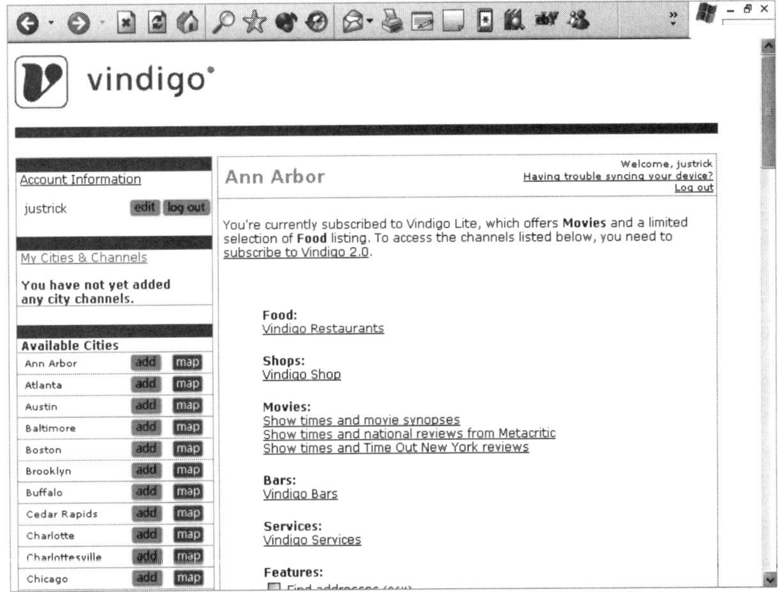

FIGURE 2-1 You manage your Vindigo account at the company's web site, where you choose desired cities and content channels for each one.

With all those steps done and choices made, all that remains is to HotSync. Each time you do, your PC will connect to Vindigo's servers, download up-to-date information, then copy it to your PDA. This is a pretty cool approach, as it eliminates the need for you to have a wireless or Internet-connected PDA. Instead, it takes advantage of your computer's existing Internet connection.

Killer Tip *If you do have a wireless or Internet-connected PDA, you can use it to download updated listings wherever you are—no PC required.*

Much of Vindigo's power lies in its street-level maps, which enable you to navigate to any destination from your current location. In fact, if you tap the Go tab, Vindigo will generate step-by-step walking directions (you can use them for driving as well, but the assumption is that if you're in a big city, you're probably on foot).

Killer Tip *When viewing Vindigo listings, look for text that's underscored with a dotted line. These are links (much like the kind you find in your web browser): when you tap one, you're taken to related information for that item, or given a map-related option if it's a street.*

FIND IT ON THE CD

Vindigo, $24.95 annual subscription
Vindigo
www.vindigo.com

11 HandMap

This Is One Map You Never Have to Fold

No one wants to look like a tourist when visiting an unfamiliar city, but it's hard to avoid that image when you walk down the street staring at a giant paper map. On the other hand, if you're interacting with your PDA, you'll look hip, sophisticated, and urbane (unless you're Dave, that is—all the PDAs in the world ain't gonna make that happen).

So skip the paper maps and load HandMap instead. The program bills itself as an "electronic street directory," but that's selling it short. With the HandMap viewer installed on your PDA, you can view high-resolution maps of just about any city or county. You can mark your current position on a map and your desired destination, and HandMap will help guide you there. You can search for a street, an intersection, a set of latitude/longitude coordinates, or even the closest restaurants, hotels, and shopping centers. You can even record notes about specific locations you've visited.

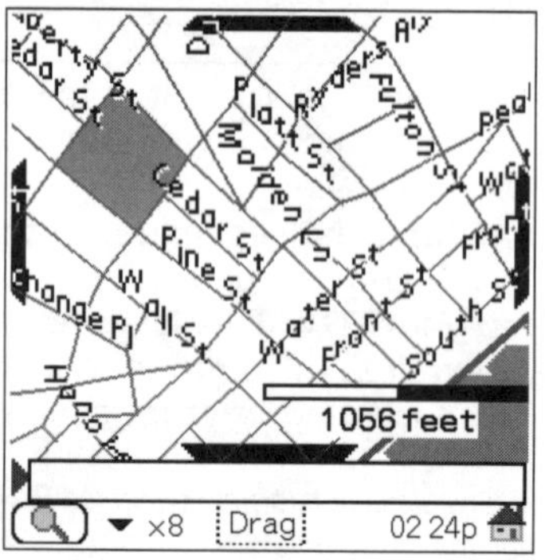

To get started with HandMap, you must first purchase the viewer, which sells for $16. Next, you'll need maps, which are available from the HandMap web site, with prices ranging from around $8 for a set of five county maps (over 3,000 U.S. counties are available) to $28 for a set of 30 U.S. cities. (The site is also home to maps of Canadian cities, Singapore, and South America.) If you're lucky enough to have a GPS receiver that works with your PDA, you can also purchase a software plug-in ($10) that adds GPS capabilities to HandMap. Instead of having to manually pinpoint your location on a map, the receiver will do it for you. (For more information on using GPS with your PDA, Rick shamefully recommends *How to Do Everything with Your GPS* (McGraw-Hill/Osborne, 2004), which he wrote.)

At this point, you're probably wondering just how useful a map can be when it's no larger than three inches—the size of your PDA's screen. Think about this: when you look at a paper map, don't you usually focus on one small area? At that point, the rest of the map becomes fairly superfluous. In any case, with HandMap you can scroll around to find the area of the map you need, then zoom in or out depending on the desired level of detail.

Killer Tip *If you're not used to electronic maps, zooming can be a hard concept to grasp. Use HandMap's onscreen zoom tool (or your PDA's up/down buttons) to experiment with magnification.*

Scrolling is best accomplished in the software's Drag mode, which is active by default but can be selected by tapping Menu | Mode | Drag. Once you've loaded a map, zoom down to around an 8x or 16x level. Now tap the center of the screen with your stylus, hold it down, and drag the stylus around. You'll see the map scroll in whatever direction you drag the stylus.

HandMap also makes it very easy to specify your location on a map. Just determine where you are, then double-tap with the stylus on that spot. You'll see a pop-up menu with three choices. Tap I Am Here to mark your location. Notice the blue X that appears. If you want to choose a destination, scroll around until you find it, double-tap again, then choose Set As Target. This time, a bull's-eye appears, designating the spot.

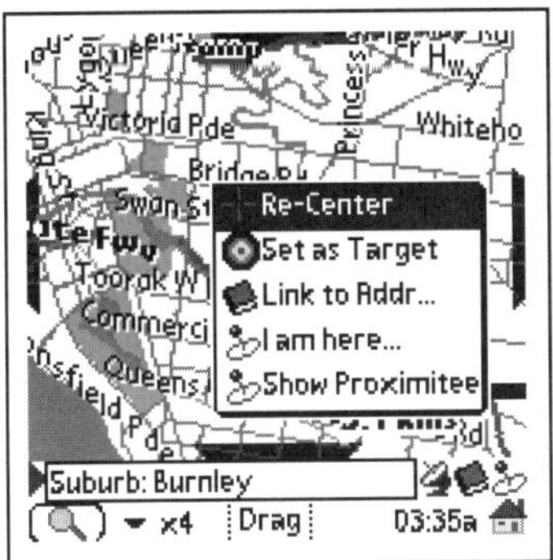

Want to search for a street name, intersection, or some other map feature? Just tap HandMap's magnifying-glass icon, choose the type of search you want, then fill in the corresponding data.

This is one of those programs that's not exactly ideal for novices, but with a little practice and experimentation, you should be able to put it to good use. Make sure to print a copy of the instruction manual, which is available on the HandMap web site: www.handmap.net/Palm/map-guide.htm.

FIND IT ON THE CD

HandMap, $16 plus maps
HandMap
www.handmap.net

12 Zagat To Go

Zagat's the Way We Like It (Uh-Huh, Uh-Huh)

While Dave's idea of fine dining is an all-you-can-eat salad bar, Rick prefers restaurants with cloth napkins, a wine list, maybe even valet parking. You probably know the best places to eat in your neck of the woods, but what about when you're traveling in an unfamiliar city—or you live in a place like New York or Chicago, where the restaurants outnumber the people? In those cases, a dining guide can come in awfully handy.

In case you're not familiar with Zagat, it began as a New York–centric dining guidebook with restaurant ratings provided by actual customers, not critics with their fancy palettes. Eventually the guide evolved and expanded, culminating with Zagat To Go 2004: a Palm OS version that includes guides for about 35 cities, each one containing food, décor, and service ratings for various upscale restaurants.

After you download the trial version (or subscribe to the service, which is continually updated and costs $24.95 per year), you'll then visit the Zagat To Go web site to choose which cities and guides to install on your PDA. (In addition to restaurant reviews, the service now includes Lifestyle and Nightlife guides—but only for a few cities.)

Using Zagat To Go is quite simple: just select the city or guide you want to view, then choose your sorting option from the pop-up menu. You can sort by favorites, most popular, type of cuisine, and so on. When you see a restaurant that's of interest, tap it to view its details, ratings, and review. Zagat ratings are on a scale of 0 to 30. Here's a quick reference key you can use to understand the listings:

- **F** Food
- **D** Décor
- **S** Service
- **C** Cost (the estimated price of dinner for one with one drink and the tip)

Killer Tip *Be sure you download and install the 14-day trial version before subscribing to Zagat To Go to make sure the service offers enough restaurants in your city—or the cities you plan to visit—to make the purchase worthwhile. For instance, it lists only about 20 restaurants for all of Detroit and the surrounding suburbs, which is where Rick lives. And Zagat serves just five locations for Dave's hometown of Colorado Springs.*

FIND IT ON THE CD

Zagat To Go 2004, $24.95 (CD or download, one-year subscription)
Zagat
www.zagat.com

13 English-French Talking Phrasebook

Foreign Languages Made Easy

We don't know about you, but we've forgotten most of the French we learned in high school (sorry, Mrs. Herman!). So it was a little embarrassing when we visited Paris and asked to buy a "purple monkey dishwasher" from a fruit stand. We could have avoided this "faux pas" (that's French for "elevator chimney") with a program like the English-French Talking Phrasebook, which includes over 250 common phrases and can actually speak them aloud! That certainly beats fumbling your way through a French dictionary and then butchering the words you're trying to pronounce. See Figure 2-2 for an example of the program's easy-to-use interface.

The Talking Phrasebook is available not only with French phrases, but also German, Spanish, and Italian. You can even get versions that work in reverse, speaking French, German, Spanish, or Italian phrases in English.

FIGURE 2-2 With the English-French Talking Phrasebook, you simply tap the word or phrase you want spoken, then tap the little speaker in the corner of the screen.

All the phrasebooks are actually databases that you load into a program called BDicty Pro (which is included in the price of the software). BDicty is a kind of general-purpose viewer that works with a large variety of dictionaries and phrasebooks. Thus, with that single program, you can carry not only the English-French Talking Phrasebook and any of its variants, but also dictionaries for 24 different languages, from Arabic to Welsh.

It's worth noting that BDicty isn't limited to language dictionaries. Beiks also carries a number of medical dictionaries, a law dictionary, a ZIP code database, and even some bible-study dictionaries.

Killer Tip *As the saying goes, the best dictionaries in life are free. The Beiks web site is home to around two dozen free dictionaries you can use with BDicty. (In fact, there's even a free version of BDicty—BDicty Lite—you can download, so the viewer and these dictionaries won't cost you a dime.) Sure, the selection is a bit eclectic, ranging from NASA Acronyms to English-French Sailing Terms, but there are genuinely useful titles like a rhyming dictionary and a name-meaning dictionary (a must for any parent-to-be).*

FIND IT ON THE CD
English-French Talking Phrasebook, $19.95 (same price for other languages)
Beiks
www.beiks.com

14 Small Talk

Parlez-Vous Palm? Let Your PDA Do the Talking

An oldie but goodie, Small Talk has been around just about forever, which is why we're always surprised more people don't know about it. This Palm OS classic is not unlike the English-French Talking Phrasebook (see App 13, "Foreign Languages Made Easy"), except that it doesn't do the talking—you do. So why bother with such a technologically outdated program? ("It doesn't even talk? Bah!") Because it has a different trick up its sleeve: two-way communication.

Let's say you're visiting Spain and don't speak a lick of Spanish (ay caramba!). Small Talk works like this: using a simple, icon-driven menu of categories, you tap until you find the commonly used question or phrase you want to say. Small Talk translates it into Spanish, then presents it on the screen in large, easy-to-read type. Then, instead of you trying to pronounce the words yourself, you just show the screen to the Spanish-speaking person. Presto: you've just communicated.

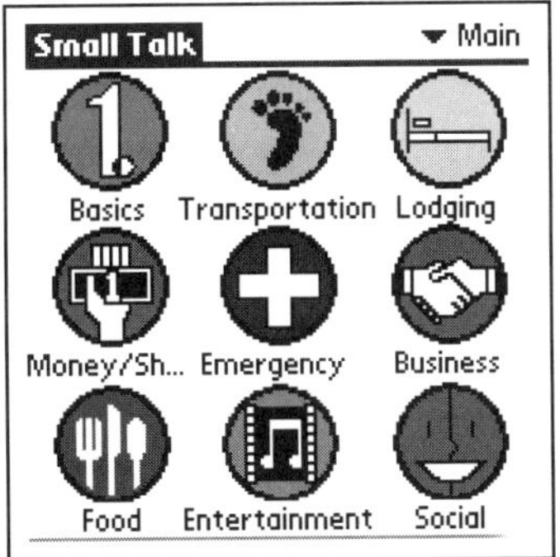

This is where most phrasebooks and dictionaries come up short: they don't allow for a reply. Sure, you've just asked where the bathroom is, but how are you supposed to understand the rapid stream of Spanish gibberish you're now hearing? When Small Talk translates a question, it includes a "Respond" button on the screen—in the person's native language! When that person taps the button, he or she is presented with a list of common or appropriate responses—again in the native language. Once tapped, the response is translated back to English for you to read. Presto: two-way communication!

Killer Tip *If you hand your PDA to a total stranger in a foreign country, it's entirely possible he or she will think it's a gift (or an easy day's petty thievery) and take off down the street with it. Solution: keep the PDA in your hand, but give the person your stylus for tapping out the reply.*

Small Talk comes with five languages: English, French, German, Italian, and Spanish. You can install just two of them to save space or all five if you're planning to hit multiple countries. Plus, the languages are interchangeable—you're not limited to translating back and forth between English and whatever. You can go from French to German, Italian to Spanish, and so on.

If you're traveling to a foreign country and don't speak the language, we can't speak highly enough of Small Talk. It's incredibly easy to use and undeniably effective at bridging the language barrier.

FIND IT ON THE CD
Small Talk, $19.95
LandWare
www.landware.com

15 Gulliver

Don't Let Your Travel Unravel

Travel is an information-intensive task these days, what with all those flight times and hotel reservations and confirmation numbers. Gulliver stores all the details of your air travel, car rentals, and hotel accommodations, thereby turning you into a more organized and better-prepared traveler.

Though you could just as easily jot the same information into a memo, there's something to be said for Gulliver's comprehensive organizational skills. It sorts trips individually; each one can contain as much flight, car, and hotel information as is necessary for the trip (helpful if your journey includes several stops). Gulliver also stores frequent-flyer ID numbers. Boasting admirably clean design, the three main data-entry screens (one each for flights, cars, and hotels) make it a snap to enter and review information.

The software incorporates listings for a multitude of airlines, airports, hotels, and car-rental agencies, but the database is out-of-date. The Colorado Springs airport and Spirit Airlines, for instance, are omitted. Fortunately, you can add new listings to any category, and edit the existing ones as well. Gulliver also saves pen strokes by auto-filling text in many fields. Thus, as you start to tap out, say, San Francisco, the software completes the entry by the time you get to the *r*.

FIND IT ON THE CD

Gulliver, $19.99
Handmark
www.handmark.com

16 Mapopolis Navigator

Door-to-Door Driving Directions Done Adroitly

This is one of the few times in this book we're going to talk about software that requires additional hardware. The software: Mapopolis Navigator, a street-level mapping program that gives you door-to-door driving directions from point A to point B. The hardware: a GPS receiver, a device that receives data from Global Positioning System satellites and uses it to determine your position. Put the two together and you can see your location on a moving map, right on your PDA screen.

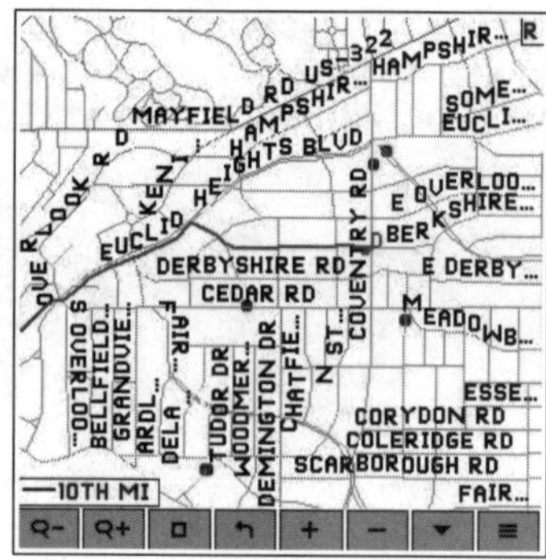

This is pretty cool stuff, but you need to understand a few things before proceeding. For starters, there's the GPS receiver. You can buy one directly from Mapopolis or investigate the products from companies like ALK, Belkin, Delorme, and Socket. Many of these come bundled with software other than Mapopolis Navigator, and you may decide to use that software instead. We don't mind—our primary purpose in this section is simply to reveal that your PDA can serve as a very capable navigation tool. The hardware and software are up to you.

That said, if your PDA has a built-in Bluetooth radio (models that do include the Palm Tungsten T series and Sony Clié UX50), we highly recommend getting a Bluetooth receiver. That way, there's no physical connection required between your PDA and the GPS—and who wants a cable flopping around your car's dashboard?

Killer Tip *Check eBay and other online sources for Bluetooth GPS receivers. Even if you buy one that's designed for Pocket PC handhelds, it should still work with your Palm OS model. That's part of the beauty of Bluetooth: it's platform-agnostic. You may be able to save big bucks by picking up a used receiver or last year's model.*

Now let's talk about Mapopolis Navigator. At press time, it was one of the most capable mapping programs available for the Palm OS, offering features like on-the-fly driving directions (meaning you choose your destination right on your PDA—no computer required—and Navigator immediately generates the directions) and voice-prompted driving directions (your PDA actually speaks to you, telling you which way to go, when to turn, and so on). But the software can be a bit confusing to use, starting with the maps themselves.

Navigator itself is free; you can download it from the Mapopolis web site or find it on this book's CD. However, it's of no use without maps. Mapopolis sells a Navigator Map Pack, which contains street maps for all of North America, for $99.95. You can also purchase individual county maps for around $10 each. We find this a really annoying approach, as it requires you to know the name of each and every county you're going to pass through on the way to your destination. Needless to say, you're probably better off buying the Map Pack—but even then you have to know which counties to load on your PDA. Blech.

You'll also want to make sure you have enough storage space on your PDA for the map files, which can be quite large. The map for Oakland County, Michigan, where Rick lives, nabs more than three megabytes' worth of memory. Fortunately, you can load maps onto a memory card, which we strongly recommend.

(For more information on using GPS with your PDA, Rick shamefully recommends *How to Do Everything with Your GPS* (McGraw-Hill/Osborne, 2004), which he wrote. It's even more shameful this time out because it's the second time he's recommended it in this chapter.)

Killer Tip *If you don't want to incur the expense of a GPS receiver or deal with the complexity of Mapopolis, you can still get door-to-door driving directions on your PDA. All you need is AvantGo (see Chapter 9), which can download directions created at the MapQuest web site.*

FIND IT ON THE CD

Mapopolis Navigator, Free (maps extra)
Mapopolis
www.mapopolis.com

The World's Best Graffiti Tip

As you know, Graffiti is the handwriting-recognition software common to all Palm OS PDAs. Some models use original Graffiti, others have stepped up to Graffiti 2. Regardless of which version runs on your PDA, there's one sure-fire way you can improve its accuracy. This is the very best Graffiti tip you'll ever learn, so pay close attention. We don't divulge this to just anybody.

Okay, ready? Here's the tip: write big.

Yep, it's nothing more complicated than that. Most of us are accustomed to scribbling fairly small print when we write on paper. Graffiti works best when you use the entire Graffiti area (top to bottom, not left to right), meaning you'll have to make your characters a bit larger than you're used to. But it's worth the reconditioning—your accuracy will improve considerably.

Chapter 3

Gone Fishin'

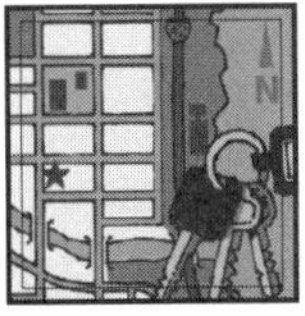

You know the future has arrived when a device the size of a deck of cards can hold a handful of Stephen King novels, the full contents of a photo album, a few of your favorite songs, and perhaps even a Hollywood movie or a television show. Don't look so surprised: your Palm OS device is great for all sorts of multimedia tricks.

And your PDA finally makes this sort of thing practical. Before Palm devices came along, for instance, a slowly growing collection of electronic books—mostly public-domain classic literature, like Voltaire's *Candide* and Sir Arthur Conan Doyle's *Sherlock Holmes* stories—existed on the Internet. But your PDA makes them convenient to read anytime, anywhere. Your Palm also makes it easy to watch movies and listen to music on an airplane or train. And just one device does it all. In this chapter, we'll check out the most exciting apps you need to make this work.

17 Palm Reader

You Already Own the Ultimate E-Book Reader

Reading your favorite books, best sellers, magazines, and more from your PDA sounds good, but it's not as easy as it sounds. Specifically, many people make the same mistake: they download a bunch of nifty e-books from some e-book web site, load them onto their Palm, then scratch their head, wondering why they can't see icons for their e-books in the Palm's main application screen. The reason, of course, is they simply don't have an e-book viewer installed. Without one, there's no way to view e-book files, which don't have their own icons.

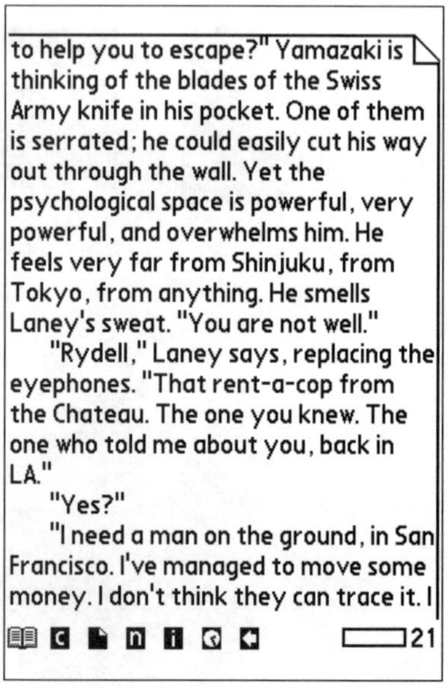

Fortunately, there are plenty of e-book viewers out there—all free or inexpensive. The best place to start is with Palm's own program, Palm Reader.

There are two versions of Palm Reader—one that's free, and a $15 Palm Reader Pro with additional features. You probably got Palm Reader with your PDA—it will either be built in or waiting for you to install it on the setup CD. If not, no fear—you can get it from www.palmdigitalmedia.com or right from the CD in this book.

If you want to, you can also try some other popular e-book choices. The most popular are CSPotRun, TealDoc, and Isilo. You can find TealDoc on the CD as well.

There are dozens of online sources for e-books, both free and commercial. Free books are usually from the public domain: either their copyrights have expired (as in the case of classic literature) or they've been written and released by authors

> to help you to escape?" Yamazaki is thinking of the blades of the Swiss Army knife in his pocket. One of them is serrated; he could easily cut his way out through the wall. Yet the psychological space is powerful, very powerful, and overwhelms him. He feels very far from Shinjuku, from Tokyo, from anything. He smells Laney's sweat. "You are not well."
>
> "Rydell," Laney says, replacing the eyephones. "That rent-a-cop from the Chateau. The one you knew. The one who told me about you, back in LA."
>
> "Yes?"
>
> "I need a man on the ground, in San Francisco. I've managed to move some money. I don't think they can trace it. I
>
> 21

not seeking compensation. There are literally thousands of titles available in the public domain.

Commercial titles aren't unlike what you'd buy in a bookstore: they've simply been converted to some electronic format and authorized for sale online. Most commercial e-books are created using a proprietary format, meaning a special viewer is required. This is primarily to prevent unauthorized distribution—unlike actual books, commercial e-books aren't meant to be loaned out or given to others. When you buy one, you're effectively buying a license to read it on your Palm device and only your Palm device. The first place you might want to look is MemoWare (www.memoware.com), as shown in Figure 3-1.

Here you can find thousands of texts divided into categories such as business, history, travel, biography, sci-fi, and Shakespeare. Whether you're looking for a collection of Mexican recipes, a Zane Grey western, a sappy love poem, or a classic work by Dickens, this is the place to start. Best of all, most are free. On the other hand, the top place to go for contemporary, mainstream fiction and nonfiction is, without a doubt, Palm's own online bookstore, Palm Digital Media (www.palmdigitalmedia.com). The site offers hundreds of books from many well-known authors.

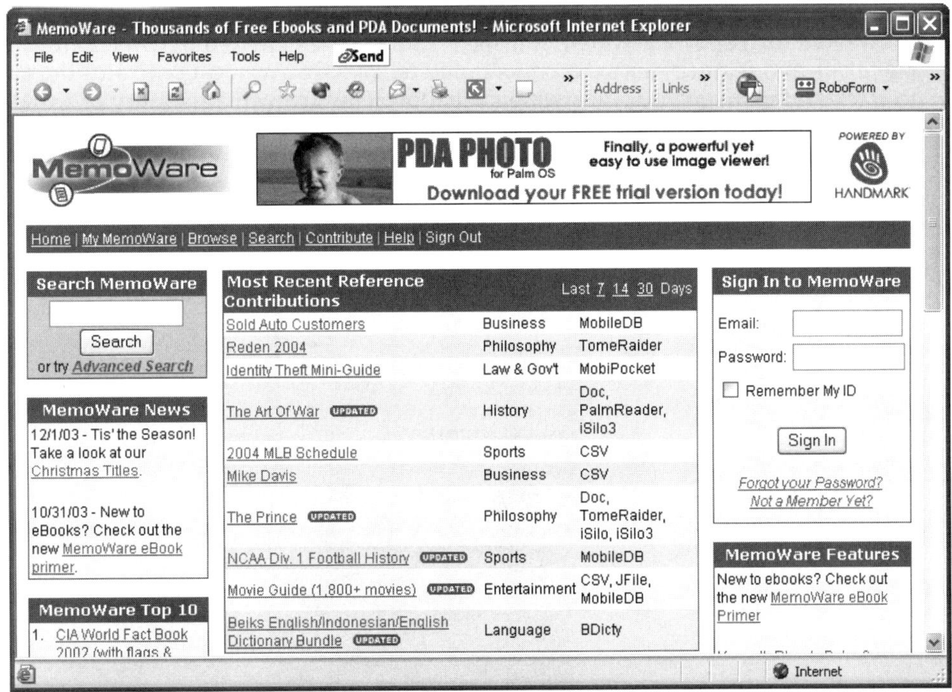

FIGURE 3-1 Web sites like MemoWare's are great resources for downloading free and inexpensive e-books.

FIND IT ON THE CD
Palm Reader, Free
Palm Digital Media
www.palmdigitalmedia.com

18 Wine Enthusiast Guide

Pick the Perfect Wine

There are few tasks in the world more onerous than selecting a wine. On the way to a party, you stop in the store and are immediately overwhelmed by enough French language and pretentious salespeople to make you want to grab a six-pack of Coke instead. Wouldn't it be great if you could bring a team of wine shopping experts with you whenever you needed to make such a decision? You can, sort of—if you have a wine reference guide on your PDA.

We like the LandWare Wine Enthusiast Guide. It was created by *Wine Enthusiast Magazine* and features an exhaustive guide to selecting wines along with the ability to track and manage your own wine collection. There's even a glossary of wine terminology—handy if you don't know your Abboccato from your Barbera.

When you start the program and see the main Guide screen, notice the Wine Selector button at the bottom right:

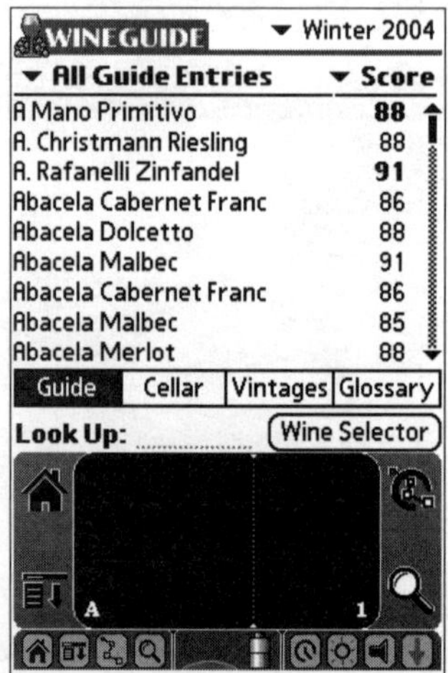

Tap it to launch the Wine Selector Wizard, which lets you choose the right wine for your occasion. You can customize a price and quality of wine, then choose a style (like red, white, or dessert wine), the grape variety (the program's built-in glossary may come in handy for this tool), and even the region from which the wine is derived.

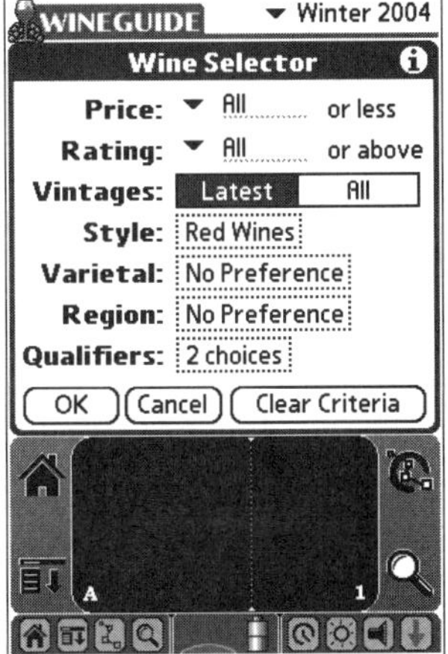

When you're done, tap OK to see your potential wine candidates.

Finally, check out the statistics for each wine. When you find a wine you are interested in, tap on it. You'll see a screen like this, which gives you lots of information about the selected wine:

FIND IT ON THE CD

Wine Enthusiast Guide, $19.95
LandWare
www.landware.com

19 BarBack Drink Guide

Mix the Perfect Drink

Do you like to imagine that you're Tom Cruise from the classic movie *Cocktail*? Or maybe, like Rick, you see yourself as Piper Perabo from *Coyote Ugly*. Let's put it this way: even if you don't fantasize about being the hero in a bartender movie, you might still want to know how to mix up some drinks. And while Bart Simpson could follow the recipes behind the bar while mixing drinks for the Mafia, you may not have that advantage. Instead, rely on your Palm to help you make your drinks.

The BarBack Drink Guide, from Town Compass, is a superb reference for making just about any kind of drink imaginable. BarBack includes 10,000 different drinks. The main screen lets you select the kind of drink category:

From there, you can fine-tune your drink from the resulting drop-down box:

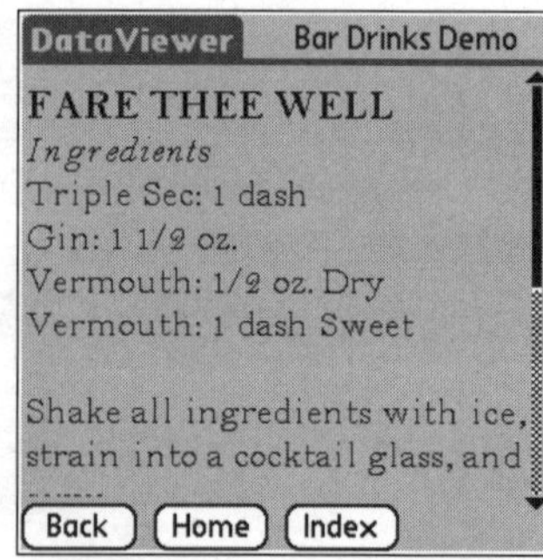

And finally, you can see a complete list of all the drinks in that category. When you find the drink you like, tap it for a complete recipe. The recipe even tells you what kind of glass to use for the most authentic look.

Want to quickly track down a certain drink by name or ingredient? You don't even have to use the browsing system. Just start BarBack and then tap the Palm's search tool (the magnifying glass in the Graffiti area) and enter the search term. You'll get a complete list of drinks that match that criteria.

FIND IT ON THE CD
BarBack Drink Guide, $9.95
Town Compass
www.pocketdirectory.com

20 MovieMentor

Choose the Perfect Movie

Seen any good movies lately? Your chances may improve with the right software on your Palm. Instead of wandering aimlessly to the local theater and hoping you make the right choice (our advice: avoid any three-word movie titles, like *Tough to Kill*, *Ready to Die*, or *Pining for Revenge*), we suggest trying a program like MovieMentor.

MovieMentor is a guide to over 2,000 in-theater and on-video flicks. The database, regularly updated and expanded each time you HotSync, is divided into 16 genres (from action to western) and spans several categories. These include recent video releases, current-run and upcoming films, and classics.

You can tap any movie to see an original—not studio-written—plot summary and basic cast/director info, and perform searches based on title, plot, director, cast, and/or notes you've added. MovieMentor also supplies its own ratings.

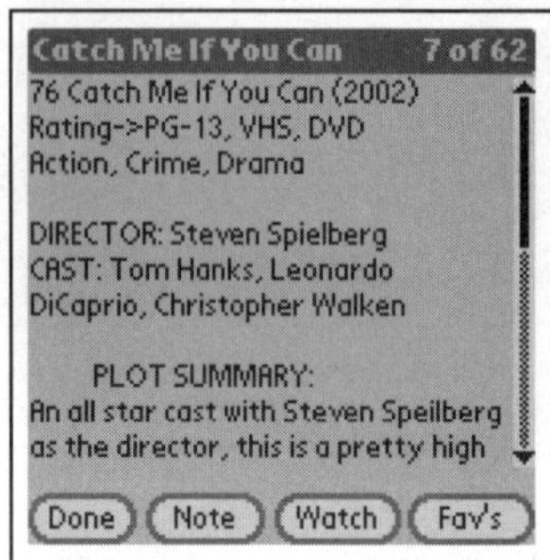

The program gives you a lot of ways to track and find movies you want to see. By using the Search button, for instance, you can search for movies with a specific actor, via a particular movie title, or with any keyword to help you locate movies of interest.

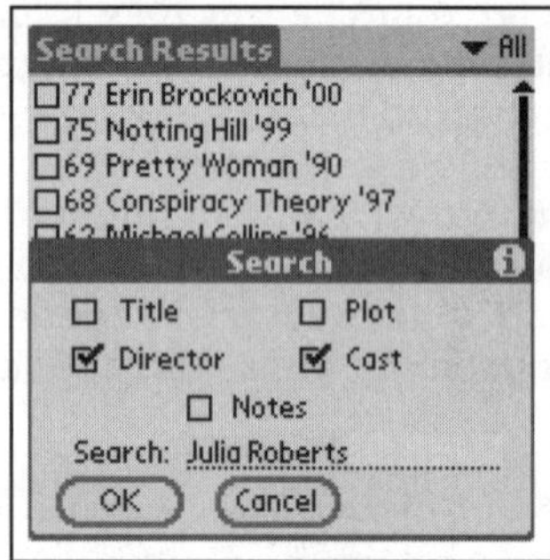

And for each of the main lists, you can create your own customized list to track the movies that you "must see."

So the next time someone asks, "Have you seen any good movies lately?" just whip out your Palm and show them your favorites list from MovieMentor.

FIND IT ON THE CD

MovieMentor, $11.95 per year
MovieMentor
www.moviementor.com

A Tiny Little Theater in Your Pocket

POWER APP

It wasn't all that long ago that watching an entire feature-length movie on a PDA would have been considered insanity. These days, though, there's no reason not to use your Palm to fire up *The Matrix* or an episode of *The Simpsons* on a long flight.

Of course, you'll want to have a lot of memory. A 128MB card is the bare minimum for watching a short TV show, and you'll probably want to have a 256MB or 512MB card for serious watching—otherwise, you'll have to break things up in multiple sections and put them on several cards.

Though there are several video players to choose from, we recommend using a program called Kinoma:

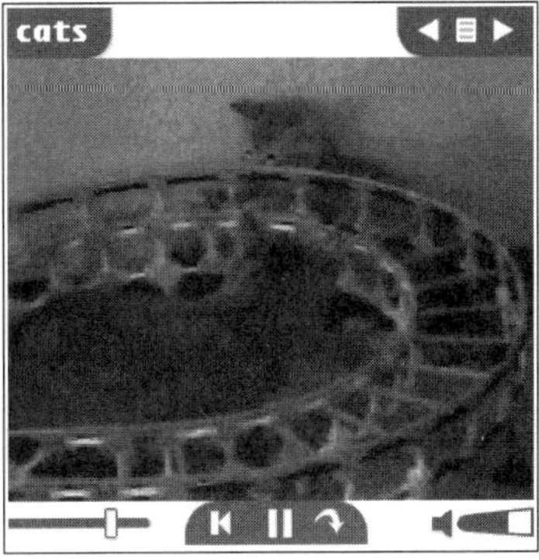

While the Kinoma viewer (the app that goes on your PDA) is free, the $30 commercial version of Kinoma comes with a desktop converter (shown in Figure 3-2) that you can use to import movies in a variety of formats, including QuickTime, MPEG-1, MPEG-4, AVI, and even Macromedia Flash.

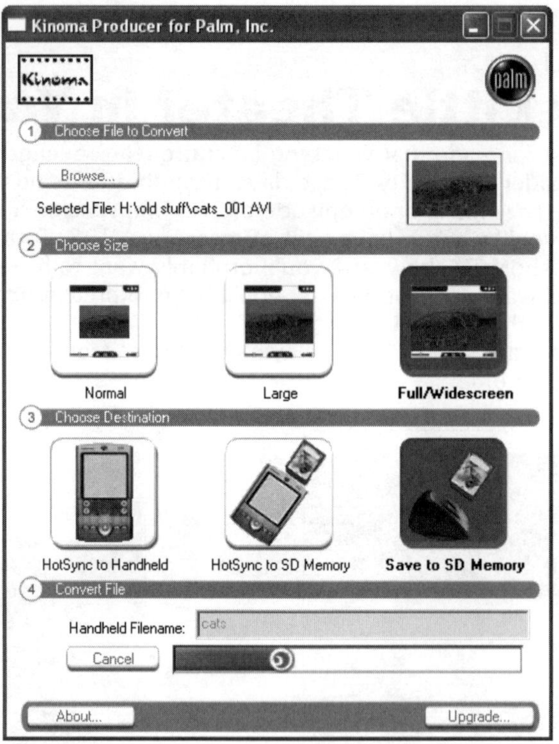

FIGURE 3-2 Kinoma Producer takes your movie file and converts it to a format suitable for the PDA.

Having a video player on your PDA is all well and good, but it's a lot like being all dressed up with nowhere to go: where do you get the movies for your PDA to begin with? The reality is that you have an embarrassment of riches when it comes to sources for video. People who watch movies on their PDAs can draw on television and videotape, DVD, their digital camcorder, and even the Internet. Here's the skinny:

- Television programs, whether live, off the air, or stored on videotape—are a common source. You might want to copy this week's episode of *Friends* or *24,* for instance, so you can watch it when you travel. You'll need some mechanism on your computer, like a composite-video-in or S-Video input, to capture analog video and store it on your PC. Some multimedia computers ship with video-capture capabilities. If your computer doesn't already have this, you can add an ATI All-in-Wonder card to your PC, which has video inputs and the necessary software to store video on a hard disk. Another alternative: Dazzle's Digital Video Creator is a USB hub that sits outside your PC and lets you capture video onto your PC via composite video or S-Video ports.

- DVD is the way most of us watch our movies these days, so it stands to reason that we'd want to be able to copy DVD to PDA. PDQ. Suppose you just rented *Terminator III* but you're going out of town before you have a chance to watch it. The problem, of course, is getting the movie off of the silver platter and onto your computer's hard disk. Since DVDs are copy-protected, this might initially seem like a hopeless task. Fret not—there are several programs around that make this possible. Programs like DVD-to-AVI (www.dvd-to-avi.com) and MovieJack (www.moviejack.org) can "rip" the content from DVD and store the movie as an AVI or MPEG file on your computer's hard drive. From there, it's a matter of synchronizing the movie with your PDA—but you should probably let your PC run overnight, because it'll take a while.
- The Internet is teeming with movies and television shows if you know where to look. Peer-to-peer services like Kazaa and LimeWire have many videos you can download from other people's computers.

Converting Movies for Kinoma

So, suppose you have a movie or two and a video player on your PDA. Think you're set? Think again. In some cases, you might really be ready to kick back and watch *Logan's Run* on your Tungsten T3. But much of the time, you still need to convert, compress, and synchronize. Not all video players recognize the same file formats, and that's where some video utilities can come in handy.

Consider this: you download a vintage Throwing Muses music video from Beestung.net with plans to play it on your Tungsten T via the Kinoma Player. When you inspect the video, though, you find that it's in a format called DIVX—and Kinoma's desktop Producer software doesn't recognize DIVX files. Game over? Nope. You just need to convert the file from DIVX to a format that Kinoma understands, like MPEG.

To do that, you'll need an intermediate utility that lets you save a video file in a different format. There is one excellent utility that we recommend without reservation: EO-Video (www.eo-video.com). EO-Video is a polished, easy-to-use video tool that lets you load files in a broad range of formats and save them as almost anything else. You can load a QuickTime file, for instance, and save it as an MPEG-1 video. More to the point, you can load WMV files—created expressly for Microsoft's Windows Media Player—and save them as general-purpose AVI or MPEG videos that Palm OS players can understand.

FIND IT ON THE CD

Kinoma, $29.95
Kinoma
www.kinoma.com

22 BalanceLog

Lose Weight and Get In Shape

Dieting and watching what you eat is hard work. You might have a plan, but it's at home...and here you are on your lunch break. What to do? If you're like Rick, you'll just assume that Twinkies are nutritious and hope for the best.

But if you're like Dave, you'll try BalanceLog, shown in Figure 3-3. It's a comprehensive weight and nutrition monitoring system for your Palm PDA. BalanceLog starts by collecting information about your nutrition and weight management goals, and then uses it to develop a complete, personalized program tailored for you. BalanceLog helps you to establish and track your nutrients, daily calorie budget, and exercise targets—and get instant feedback on your progress. The program lets you set weight management and nutrition goals, access a database of more than 300 exercises and 4,000 foods, including brand-name foods and menu items from national restaurant chains, and accurately track your incoming and outgoing calories.

FIND IT ON THE CD

BalanceLog, $46
HealtheTech
www.healthetech.com

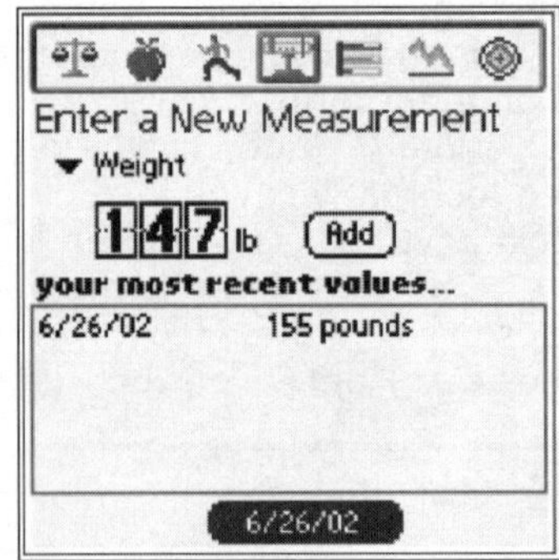

FIGURE 3-3 BalanceLog is a powerful, portable weight and nutrition monitoring system that you can carry on your Palm.

23 Star Pilot Plus

Follow the Stars

"My God," David Bowman said in *2001: A Space Odyssey,* "It's full of stars." While he was referring to the black, rectangular monolith that was orbiting Jupiter, the same can be said of your PDA—with the right software. Using a star tracker like Star Pilot Plus, from Star Pilot Technologies, you can put a planetarium in your pocket and reference it anywhere, anytime—at home, at work, or when you're hauling the telescope into the backyard.

As you can see next, Star Pilot Plus is a gorgeous program that's sure to be a favorite of any backyard astronomer. It has a database of about 1,500 stars and 88 constellations. And you don't have to see them all onscreen; if you live in a brightly lit urban area, you can switch to city mode, which blocks all but the highest magnitude objects so you can more accurately predict what's visible in the night sky.

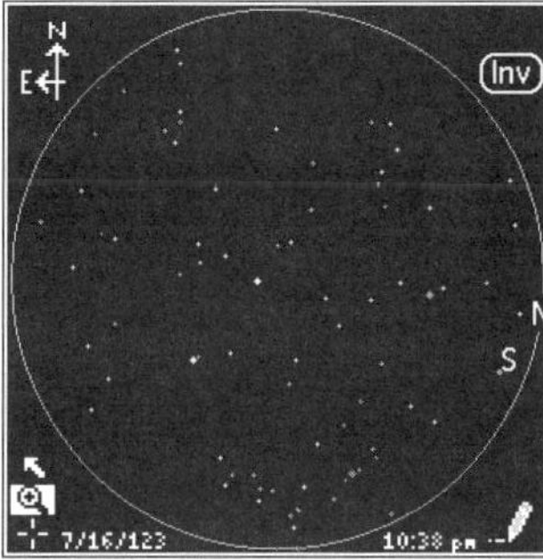

When you first install Star Pilot Plus, it may not include the Location Manager—especially if you download it from the Web instead of installing it from the book's CD-ROM. But it's important to get the Location Manager, since it is a comprehensive database of U.S. cities that tells the program where you are (or where you want to simulate viewing the sky from). If it's not in your install file, get the Location Manager from this URL: www.star-pilot.com/locmgr. Then select your location from the list.

When you first start Star Pilot Plus, you'll see a screen like this one:

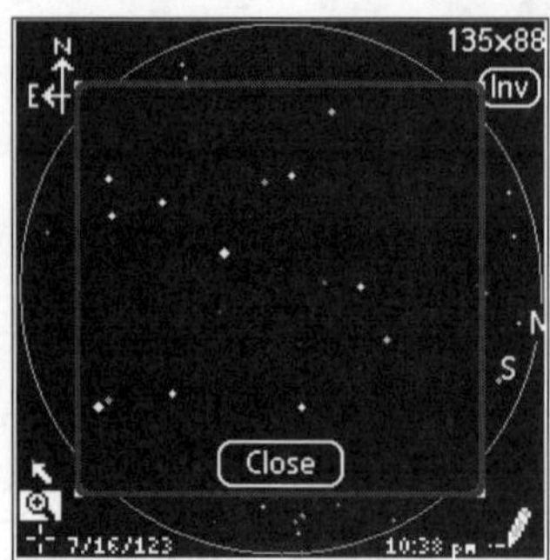

Killer Tip *For best results, you'll want to turn on the color magnitude display. Choose Options | Magnitudes from the menu and tap Color Objects, then tap OK.*

Also notice the tools in the lower-left corner of the screen. You can zoom in for a better view by tapping the magnifying glass or use the crosshair tool to find out information about a specific celestial body by tapping directly on it.

FIND IT ON THE CD
Star Pilot Plus, $19.95
Star Pilot Technologies
www.star-pilot.com

24 TealAuto

Manage Your Motorcoach

If you're like us, you track your oil changes in only the vaguest of terms—"Did I change the oil this year yet?" you wonder. What's the fuel efficiency of the car? Somewhere between 10 and 30 miles per gallon, no doubt. At least, that was the way we used to be before we started using our PDA as a powerful automotive manager.

There are a number of auto management programs around, but we think that TealAuto is the most elegant and complete automotive database we've seen. It has a smart and colorful interface with easy-to-use tabs for tracking fuel efficiency, business trips, and the full gamut of maintenance and service. TealAuto is highly customizable; you can create a custom service schedule for your car as well as enter personalized entries in the program's many databases—that's handy for selecting details like local gas stations, preferred fuel grades, and specific maintenance items from pick lists.

TealAuto lets you track multiple vehicles, export reports to your PC, and it even has a clever "meter minder" alarm so you can avoid costly parking tickets. The only thing it doesn't do is change the oil; you'll have to do that yourself.

Here you can see the program's main interface:

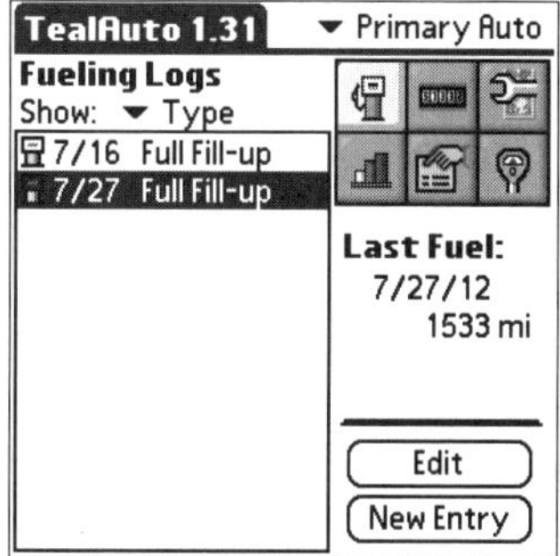

The tabs—buttons, actually—at the top right of the screen switch you among the program's many modes. Start with tracking your fuel stops. If you remember to enter how much gas you put in your car every time you fill up, you'll get a precise reading of your fuel efficiency, which should stay steady over time.

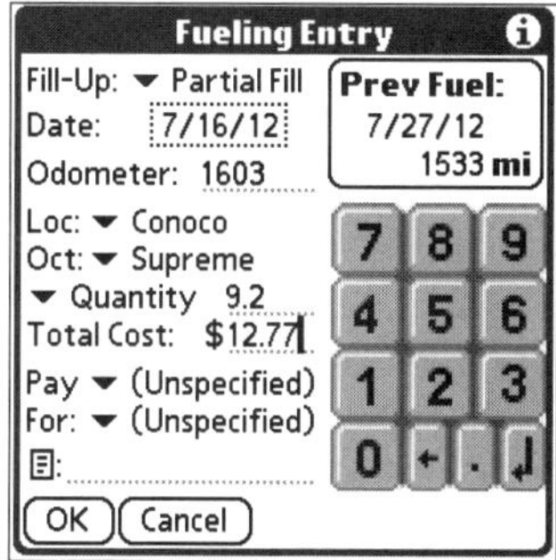

If your efficiency goes down suddenly, that's an indication there's something wrong with your car. So using TealAuto for just a few moments a week can save you money on auto maintenance in the long run.

FIND IT ON THE CD

TealAuto, $16.95
TealPoint Software
www.tealpoint.com

25 SplashPhoto

A Photo Album in Your Pocket

What's the first thing you do when you meet an old friend and the subject turns to family? No doubt, you pull your wallet out of your pocket and start showing off your pictures. The new, twenty-first century way to do that, though, is to show off pics on your Palm. It only makes sense—your pictures are probably digital already anyway (you do have a digital camera, right?) so it should be a simple matter to copy your favorites to your Palm.

But what if your particular PDA doesn't have a picture viewer built in? Is it still possible to keep a digital photo album in your pocket? You bet. With the right photo viewer software, you'll never be without a picture of your spouse, kids, cats, or other loved ones. The process is quite simple: electronic images on your desktop PC are converted to the right format, then installed when you HotSync. Then you load up your viewer and, well, view 'em.

Many programs enable you to view images on your PDA, some of them quite similar in their form and function. Here are some of the most popular programs:

- **AcidImage** This is an excellent photo viewer that reads plain old JPG images off your PDA's expansion card, so you don't have to use a cumbersome desktop conversion program first. Just drag and drop JPG images from the PC onto your Clié.
- **HandStory Suite** This multifaceted program displays e-book doc files, web clips, memos, and digital images. The desktop transfer process is very elegant; just right-click an image on the desktop and choose Save to Palm from the menu.
- **SplashPhoto** A somewhat "traditional" photo album, SplashPhoto relies on a desktop converter to crop and edit images down to size for the Palm's screen. It also reads pure JPG images.
- **Photogather** Similar to SplashPhoto, Photogather has a desktop converter as well. Beware, though: Photogather sends full-resolution images to the Palm instead of shrinking them to fit on the screen—and that can eat up a lot of memory very quickly.

Indeed, SplashPhoto is our favorite, and you can find it on the included CD-ROM. SplashPhoto starts in Windows, where the SplashPhoto Desktop displays all of the images stored on your PDA, both in internal memory and on expansion cards. Want to add a photo to the PDA? Just drag and drop it into the Desktop, and it'll appear on your PDA after the next HotSync—complete with text notes and categorized however you like.

On the Palm itself, you can view images by tapping on them or set up a slideshow that'll display images from any selected category.

SplashPhoto can display JPEG, BMP, and GIF images without any conversion process, so you can pop a memory card from your camera into the PDA and immediately view pictures. There's no limit to how many pictures or categories SplashPhoto can handle, and you can do handy tricks like recategorizing a batch of images in a single step from either the Palm or the desktop. SplashPhoto even keeps track of multiple memory cards without getting confused. And then there's the best news of all: when you copy images to the PDA, you can resize them to the size of the PDA screen or copy full-resolution images. SplashPhoto handles a mish-mash of fit-to-screen and large digital images with aplomb, and you can view big images at full size and pan around to see details, or fit the image to the screen. What more could you ask for? So fill up your PDA with pictures now, and we can compare families the next time you run into one of us.

Killer Tip *We're also fond of AcidImage, so look for a demo of that program on the CD-ROM as well.*

FIND IT ON THE CD
SplashPhoto, $29.95
SplashData
www.splashdata.com

26 AeroPlayer

The Ultimate MP3 Player

Does your PDA have an audio jack for stereo headphones? Then it can do double duty as a digital music player. That's right—not only can you read e-books, manage your schedule, and watch movies on your Palm, but you can use it as a music player as well. Kind of a cutting-edge Walkman.

Your PDA may even have come with its own MP3 player, but there are others available as well. And, as is so often the case, add-in MP3 players are often better than whatever came in the box to begin with.

Our favorite digital music player for the Palm is a little program called AeroPlayer, from Aerodrome Software. We've placed a copy of AeroPlayer on the book's CD-ROM.

One of the best things about AeroPlayer is its ability to work with MP3 and Ogg Vorbis files. While Ogg Vorbis might sound like some alien species from *Star Trek*, it's really a highly efficient alternative to MP3 files and one that is getting rather popular. It also includes an equalizer that you can set and forget or configure manually with five independent frequency bands:

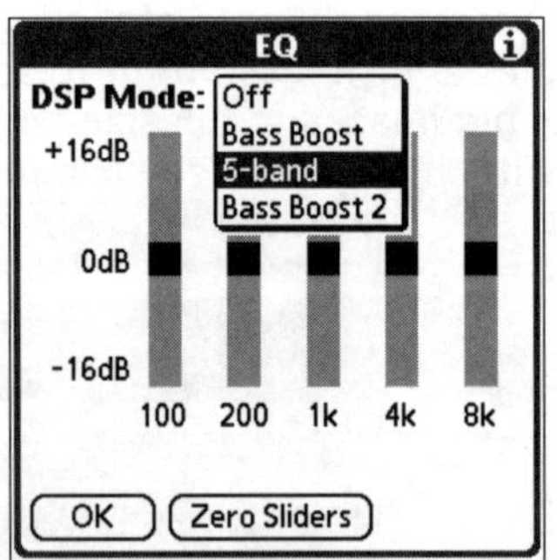

The single best feature, though, is AeroPlayer's support for skins. Skins are files that can change the entire look and operation of a program. Since you can apply skins to AeroPlayer, you can radically change the way the program looks at the tap of a stylus. There are many prebuilt skins available for AeroPlayer—here's what a few look like:

Finally, AeroPlayer multitasks quite elegantly with other Palm applications—start the player and switch to your e-book reader to read a book with background music, for instance. That's not too unusual, since many programs have such a feature. But perform a Command stroke in the Graffiti area (a diagonal stroke up and to the right) and you'll get access to its command panel, where you can pause, change tracks, and even adjust the volume—all without leaving your second application.

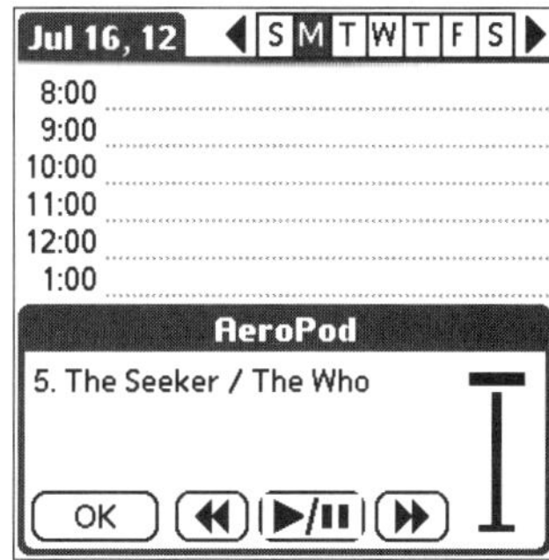

FIND IT ON THE CD

AeroPlayer, $14.95
Aerodrome Software
www.aerodrome.us

27 Pocket Cook Deluxe

Unleash Your Inner Julia Child

When the PC was brand new back in the early 1980s and no one really knew why anyone would want a computer in their home, computer companies kept insisting that they'd be great tools for managing recipes. That's right—all they could think of was the fact that people might want to copy their collection of Christmas cookie and BBQ recipes to a computer.

Times have changed. These days, we have lots of things to use computers for, but believe it or not, recipe management is a really cool thing to do with your PDA. You can carry it into the kitchen and actually use it to make something at mealtime. And for this kind of project, we like to use Pocket Cook Deluxe from The Electronic Frontier.

Pocket Cook Deluxe has two components: a desktop program that runs in Windows and a PDA application that synchronizes with it. After installing the program, you add the Palm program to your PDA by opening the Pocket Cook Deluxe program on your PC and choosing Download | Download Software to Palm from the program's menu.

The Palm program lets you search for recipes by name, ingredient, or directions:

When you find the recipe you want, you can look at the ingredients or cooking directions:

Killer Tip *Want to make the recipe for more or fewer people? Tap the button at the bottom of the screen that indicates how many people the recipe serves. You can enter any number, tap Recalc, and the recipe automatically adjusts all the measurements accordingly.*

FIND IT ON THE CD
Pocket Cook Deluxe, $19.95
The Electronic Frontier, Ltd.
www.pocket-cook.com

28 TealPaint

Paint a Pretty Picture

You're probably wondering why you might want to paint on a handheld computer so small that it fits in your pocket. Well, in the world of computers, the answer is often "because you can." Programmers have never let something as silly as a technical limitation get in the way of doing something, so when PDAs first came out, programmers seemed to scramble to become the first to create a paint program for their favorite handheld PC.

But, aside from that admittedly flippant answer, the capability to sketch things out on your Palm is a handy feature. You can draw a map to sketch the way to lunch, outline a process, or design a flowchart. You can also just doodle—use the PDA as a high-tech Etch a Sketch for those boring times when you're waiting for the train or pretending to take notes in a meeting. Perhaps most importantly, you can draw on top of pictures you've stored on your Palm, giving you the ability to annotate images and add captions.

Believe it or not, a variety of painting and drawing applications are available for the Palm. Indeed, if you're an adventurous sort of person, search the archives of a software web site like www.palmgear.com for painting programs, and you'll be amazed by what you find. Nonetheless, our hands-down favorite is a program called TealPaint, from TealPoint Software:

Certainly the most full-featured paint program for the Palm, TealPaint pretty much does it all. The program has a complete set of painting tools, including lines, shapes, fill tools, an eraser, and a variety of brushes. The program starts you in this screen, which displays thumbnail images of your pictures and lets you view, edit, or animate them. Using TealPaint, you can copy and paste selections of your image, not just within the same picture, but in any picture in your database.

TealPaint is also an animation tool. Yes, you can use TealPaint to create animations by playing all the images in a particular database in sequence. To create a simple bouncing ball, for instance, make a series of images in which the ball moves a bit in each successive image. Then tap the Anim button and tap the first picture in your series.

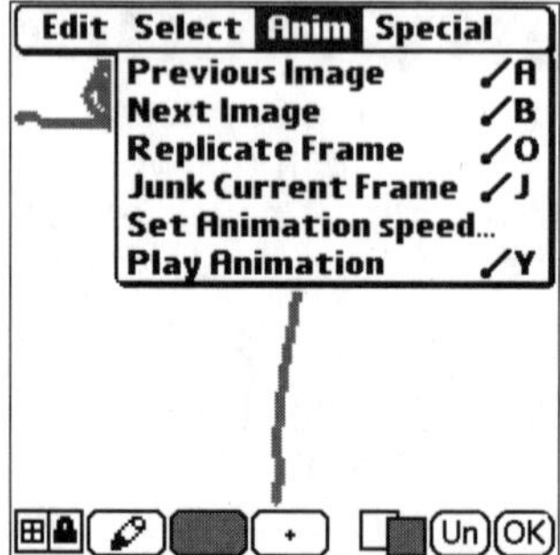

Painting on your Palm is fun and can possibly be productive, but you need to remember a couple of limitations. Palm models vary in resolution from 160×160 pixels all the way up to 480×320 pixels. The more pixels you have, the better, but even the highest-resolution devices don't give you a lot of room in which to draw. After your images are transferred to a PC, you'll find that they're still quite small. So, drawing something on the PDA you later plan to export to, say, a PowerPoint presentation, generally isn't a practical plan.

And even more important, few paint programs support printing directly from the Palm, and not all even let you transfer completed art back to the PC. That means, in some cases, what you draw on the screen pretty much stays on the screen. If you *can* print your work of art, it'll print just as rough and jagged on paper as it looked onscreen.

FIND IT ON THE CD

TealPaint, $17.95
TealPoint Software
www.tealpoint.com

Abracadabra—Was That Your Card?

Everyone loves a good magic trick. And lots of people even seem to like a bad magic trick. But don't worry—what we've got for you here is a collection of good tricks. If you are in the habit of carrying your Palm with you no matter where you go, you might appreciate having a small stockpile of magic tricks on your device for parties and other situations where you need a little icebreaker.

There are all sorts of easy-to-do card tricks, memory tricks, and number-manipulation tricks available for the Palm. Here are some of the best we've found:

- **PDA Magic** From a hand of six cards, PDA Magic removes the one card that you're thinking of. It's a clever trick—but easy to figure out.
- **PicKaCard** PicKaCard is a simple magic trick you can do for your friends. Give your PDA to someone, asking them to choose a card. When you get the PDA back, you can, after a moment's meditation, tell your victim what card was chosen. The trick is hard to figure out, but you learn the secret if you register.

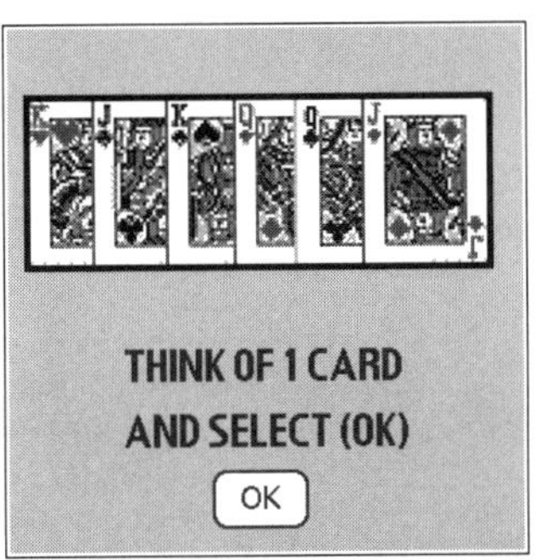

- **Magic Trick Game Pack** This is a collection of card, number, and memory tricks. Topsy-Turvy, for instance, lets you tell your audience exactly what card they were thinking of from a collection on the Palm screen. SpiritWriter lets you predict a three-digit number in someone's mind.
- **PalmMagic II** Found on the CD-ROM, this trick lets you tell your audience which of a small hand of cards they were thinking of. It's not something your

audience is likely to figure out—as long as you do it once and then simply put your Palm away.

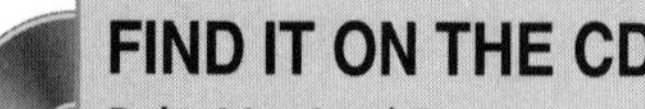

FIND IT ON THE CD

PalmMagic, $5
Ken Duncan
www.palmgear.com

30 Audible.com

Can You Hear Me Now?

Calling all fans of audio books, National Public Radio, and the *Wall Street Journal!* Thanks to Audible.com (see Figure 3-4), you can now get your fix in digital format. Audible.com lets you download more than 30,000 hours of spoken-word programs, including fiction, lectures, radio shows, and newspapers directly to your Palm device so you can listen as if they were digital music files. We can't say enough good things about Audible.com; the selection is outstanding, and the cost is far less than that of purchasing old-fashioned books on tape. Forget books on tape and sign up for this digital library pronto.

FIGURE 3-4 Audible.com is one-stop shopping for audio books you can hear on your Palm.

Though you can purchase Audible.com content piecemeal—bought separately, fiction and nonfiction titles average 35 percent cheaper than their cassette-tape counterparts—the better bet is to sign up for one of two AudibleListener plans. For $14.95 per month, you can download one audio book and one subscription-based offering, such as NPR's *This American Life.* Pony up $19.95 per month, and the deal includes two audio books.

It's easy to browse and shop for your content at www.audible.com. But remember—first, you must download and install AudibleManager, a Windows-only program that shuttles downloads from the service to your PDA. Then peruse the site to add selections to your shopping cart. Once purchased, the choices show up in your permanent online library. A few clicks transfer the content to your PC, where AudibleManager intercepts it. You must manually transfer books to your Palm, but AudibleManager can synchronize with your online library to fetch subscription content automatically. Just plug in your

PDA, and you can wake up to the *New York Times* preloaded for the ride to work—check out a view of Audible.com on your Palm:

One caveat: Audible.com uses no fewer than five proprietary audio formats, each with a different sound quality and file size. Most Audible.com titles don't come in every format, and most portable players (like the Palm) don't support them all. This awkward approach notwithstanding, Audible.com scores with its terrific library of reasonably priced content. If you like the spoken word, you'll love this service.

FIND IT ON THE CD

Audible.com, Free (but content available on subscription basis)
Audible
www.audible.com

Chapter 4

Fun and Games

All work and no play makes, well, Dave. But there's nothing dull about your PDA, which is capable of some truly excellent fun. This includes not only practical fun, like the golf scorecard program that kicks off this chapter, but also classic boardgames like Monopoly, classic computer games like SimCity, and classic parlor games like pool. Whether you've got five minutes to kill while waiting for a taxi or five hours on a coast-to-coast flight, you'll find plenty of entertainment on your PDA.

31 IntelliGolf

To the Links, Caddie!

Rick is not a golfer. Dave is not a golfer. So you're probably thinking, "Right, like I'm going to take golf advice from two guys who don't know a sand wedge from a sandwich." Hey, it's okay with us if you don't try IntelliGolf—but you'll be missing out on the coolest scorecard program in all of recorded golf history (which goes back more than *ten* years!).

Calling IntelliGolf a scorecard program belies its capabilities. While it can indeed keep score for up to five players per round, it can also track shots for every club, manage wagering games (such as skins, scramble, and point quota), and show you statistics and graphs based on your performance over time. It also enables you to download course information—hole par, handicap, and length—for over 18,000 courses, so you don't have to input all that stuff manually before your round. Just download the course from the IntelliGolf web site, HotSync your PDA, and hit the links.

The Birdie Edition of IntelliGolf includes a Windows component (see Figure 4-1) that synchronizes with your PDA and gives you a more complete overview of your rounds, statistics, and so on. You can also print your scorecards and post them around the office for bragging rights (or some good-natured ribbing—"Look, Dave shot a 397!").

Killer Tip *If you don't need or want the Windows component, you can save $10 by purchasing IntelliGolf Par Edition, which includes only the Palm OS software. All the other features are the same, and your data still gets backed up when you HotSync.*

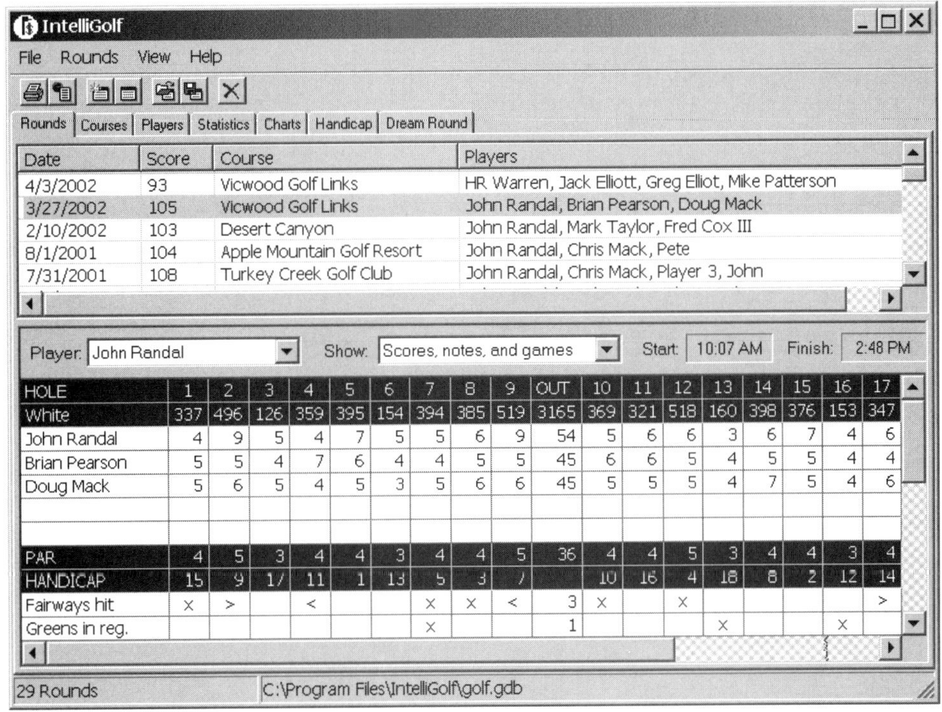

FIGURE 4-1 When you HotSync, IntelliGolf Birdie Edition transfers all the details of your round from your PDA to your PC, where you can track your progress, print scorecards, and more.

The latest version of IntelliGolf has one particularly advanced feature that merits attention. If you have a GPS receiver that works with your PDA, IntelliGolf can compute the exact distance from your location on the fairway to the green. Armed with that information, you can select the best club for your shot and, hopefully, shave some strokes from your score.

To use this IntelliGPS technology, you need two things: a GPS receiver that's compatible with your PDA, and GPS coordinates for the course you're playing. The latter are included with the course info you download from the IntelliGolf web site, though not all courses have been updated with the necessary GPS data. For those that aren't, you can record the coordinates yourself during your first round of play—then you'll have them for all future rounds.

As for the GPS receiver, there are countless choices. If your PDA has a built-in (or even add-on) Bluetooth radio, your best bet is a Bluetooth GPS. That's because it's wireless, meaning you could leave the receiver strapped to your golf bag and still obtain coordinates on your PDA from up to 30 feet away. ALK, Belkin, Delorme, and Socket are among the GPS companies that offer Bluetooth receivers. They also offer wired solutions for non-Bluetooth PDAs.

FIND IT ON THE CD
IntelliGolf 7.0 Birdie Edition, $39.95
Karrier Communications
www.intelligolf.com

32 SimCity

Manage Your Own City

Dave's definition of a fun game is one in which things "blow up real good." Rick prefers thinking to carnage, hence his fondness for SimCity—a thinking person's game in the truest sense. You've probably heard of the eponymous desktop classic, which in the late '80s just about ruined personal productivity with its highly addictive mix of city building and management. (City building and management? Sounds about as much fun as a root canal, but trust us when we say it's thoroughly engaging. It wouldn't be a classic otherwise.)

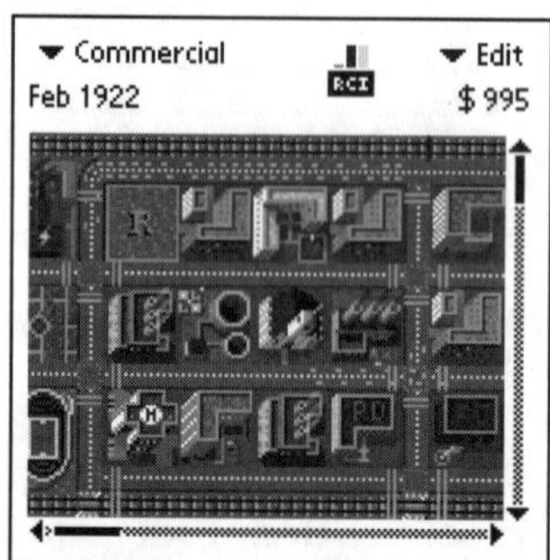

SimCity for Palm OS is a licensed version of the original, meaning it looks and plays exactly the same. You start with an empty stretch of land; it's up to you to build roads, power plants, residential areas, police and fire departments, and so on. In other words, you're pretty much a deity. Once teeny little sim-citizens start moving into your mini-metropolis, you shift gears from god to mayor (same difference), working overtime to keep everyone happy. That means keeping taxes low while still generating enough revenue for new roads, more power plants, the occasional football stadium—get the idea?

Killer Tip *If you just can't make ends meet and don't mind a little harmless cheating, write "FUND" (without the quotation marks) in the Graffiti area to get an extra $10,000. Interestingly, that's the exact same cheat used in the original desktop version of the game. Just be sure you don't go to this particular cheat well too often, or your city will get hit by an earthquake!*

If things are humming along nicely (or even if they're not), you can put on the god shoes again and see how your city deals with a "natural" disaster: fire, flood, and maybe a visit from good old Godzilla. Mwa ha ha ha! (Don't be afraid to indulge your god complex—you can always rebuild after a catastrophe.)

All this should come as good news to SimCity fans (and simulation fans in general). Now for the bad news. Because the game has to squish into your PDA's relatively small screen, you don't get to see as much of your city at a time, so you wind up scrolling around quite a bit—which kills some of the fun. Worst still, as of press time the game wasn't compatible with Palm OS 5. If you own a model that has OS 5 or later and want to play SimCity, e-mail the developers (info@ateliersoftware.com) and bug them to get moving on an update. We're eagerly awaiting a high-resolution version with sound effects and OS 5 support. It's long overdue.

FIND IT ON THE CD

SimCity, $29.95
Atelier Software
www.ateliersoftware.com

33 Merriam-Webster Crossword Challenge

Big Book of Crosswords—In Your Little PDA

One of the reasons we're so fond of reading books on our PDAs (see Chapter 3) is convenience: it's a lot easier to fit a PDA in your pocket than a copy of Stephen King's latest hardcover. Same goes for crossword puzzles: we love doing them, but who wants to carry around a big book of 'em? (Sure, there's always the newspaper, but it gives you just one puzzle, and then you wind up with ink on your fingers, plus they're impossible to open when you're packed into a coach seat, and there's never a pen around when you need one...sigh. Oh, don't get us wrong, we love newspapers, especially ones with Dave Barry, but...where were we?)

Merriam-Webster Crossword Challenge packs several hundred puzzles into your PDA and wraps them in an attractive, easy-to-use interface. Tap any square to see the "across" clue for that word; tap it again to see the "down" clue. You write letters using Graffiti, just as you would when entering other data. There's no onscreen keyboard, however, so if you haven't mastered Graffiti yet, now's the time.

The game lets you play at three different skill levels. The puzzles themselves don't change; rather, each level includes a different number of hints (tap the question mark icon to reveal the highlighted letter) and "verifies" (used to see if the letter in the selected square is correct—if not, it gets erased). The Easy level gives you ten verifies and five hints, Medium gives you five verifies and three hints, and Hard makes you figure out the puzzle the old-fashioned way.

There's just one little wrinkle with this otherwise excellent game: it doesn't support memory cards. The two files required for the high-resolution color version of Crossword Challenge require nearly 2MB of memory—pretty steep if your PDA has only 16MB total. (See the following Killer Tip as well as the sidebar "Make Any Game Run from a Memory Card" for ways around that problem.)

Killer Tip *We normally advise people to stay away from software that comes on memory cards, as you usually get less than what you pay for. One exception is Mobile Digital Media's Merriam-Webster Crossword Puzzles & Word Challenges (www.gomdm.com), which includes not only Crossword Challenge, but also three other great word games: Link Letters, Text Twist (one of Rick's personal favorites—see "A Game That Boggles the Mind," later in this chapter), and WhatWord. This foursome would cost you about $60 if purchased separately—the card sells for $30 and keeps your PDA's memory free for other stuff. Such a deal!*

Until Crossword Challenge came along, we'd forgotten how much fun crossword puzzles can be. In fact, we'd be remiss if we didn't mention another terrific title: Stand Alone's Crossword Puzzles for Palm OS (www.standalone.com). It costs $5 more than Crossword Challenge, but it has one important additional feature: it works with puzzles you can download from newspaper web sites across the country. Thus, you not only get a bunch of crosswords from the guy who writes them for the *Washington Post,* you get access to a virtually unlimited supply of extras. Check out the demo—it's on the CD!

FIND IT ON THE CD

Merriam-Webster Crossword Challenge, $14.95
Hexacto
www.hexacto.com

Make Any Game Run from a Memory Card

Okay, so you're dying to play a game like Merriam-Webster Crossword Challenge, but you just don't have 2MB of memory to spare on your PDA. If only the game could run from a memory card! (Many games can—check the documentation—but there are exceptions.) You need a utility like PowerRUN (www.palmgear.com), which effectively fools the Palm Operating System into thinking that programs stored on a card are actually in internal memory. While it works quite seamlessly once it's up and running, PowerRun is something of an advanced user's tool, so be sure to follow the instructions carefully.

34 The Emperor's Mahjong

Can't We All Just Get Mahjong?

The traditional game of mahjong is played with four people seated around a square table, with dozens of ceramic tiles in the middle. Okay, how do you turn that into something you play on your PDA? In the case of The Emperor's Mahjong, you change the rules a bit. (Hey, he's the Emperor, he can do what he wants!)

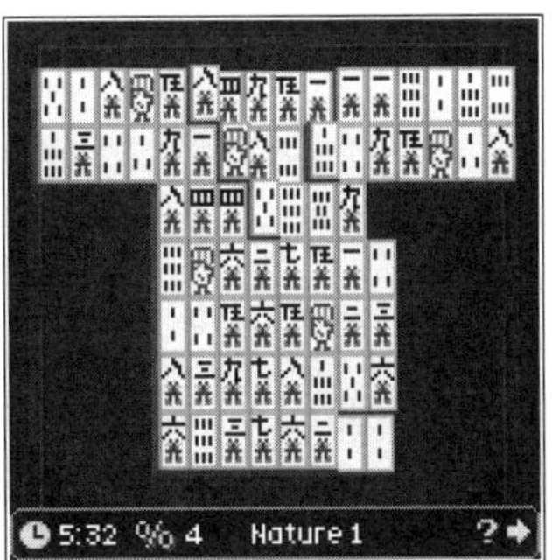

The game works like this: you're presented with a board containing dozens of tiles. You have six minutes in which to clear at least 100 tiles from the board, which is done by tapping identical pairs (or pairs belonging to like families). Needless to say, this is a bit different from traditional mahjong, which has more in common with gin rummy.

Okay, so maybe the Emperor had a little too much sake in classifying this a mahjong game. It's still pretty fun—try the demo and see for yourself.

Killer Tip *Interested in a more traditional mahjong game? Check out MahJongKing (www.toysoft.ca), in which you play against three computer opponents and utilize standard mahjong rules. Try the demo—it's on the CD!*

FIND IT ON THE CD
The Emperor's Mahjong, $14.95
Hexacto
www.hexacto.com

35 Trivial Pursuit

Honey, I Shrunk Trivial Pursuit!

Most people have a love/hate relationship with Trivial Pursuit, the 1980s trivia game that once and for all separated the smart people from, well, Dave. Actually, Rick's no champ when it comes to trivia, either, but he'll blow you off the tennis court, so there.

Handmark's Trivial Pursuit re-creates the beloved game on your PDA, allowing you to play it anywhere, anytime, with up to five other players. This version includes over 1,600 multiple-choice and true-false questions (some covering very recent events, such as the SARS epidemic) in six familiar categories: Arts and Entertainment, History, Sports and Leisure, Science and Nature, People and Places, and Wildcard. The goal remains the same: answer questions correctly to fill your game piece with wedges and prove you're the smartest one in the group.

If you'd rather dispense with the game board and just test your trivia knowledge, Trivial Pursuit offers a Flash mode in which you answer questions in order to move up the rungs of a ladder. The first player to reach the top and answer the final question correctly wins the game. Regardless of which mode you choose, Trivial Pursuit serves up the occasional "trivia fact," an informative bit of info related to the question you just answered.

Killer Tip *Tap the magnifying-glass icon to zoom in on the game board. Tap it again to zoom out and see the entire board. Tap the little dancing-i icons to see additional gameplay tips.*

FIND IT ON THE CD

Trivial Pursuit, $29.99
Handmark
www.handmark.com

36 Battleship, Scrabble, and Yahtzee

Scrabble, Yahtzee, Battleship—It's Like the '70s All Over Again

Back in the '70s, cable TV didn't exist, VCRs were an expensive luxury item, and the Internet wasn't even known as the Internet. (It was called the Arpanet, and it was used primarily to connect government and university mainframe computers. There's your trivia for the day.) Small wonder boardgames were so popular—there was nothing else to do!

Fortunately, many of these games are just as fun today as they were decades ago—and now you don't need a kitchen table (or even other players) to play them. Classics like Scrabble, Yahtzee, and Battleship are available for your PDA, and they're not just clones, either—they're licensed versions of the originals, so they look and play just like you remember. Take a look:

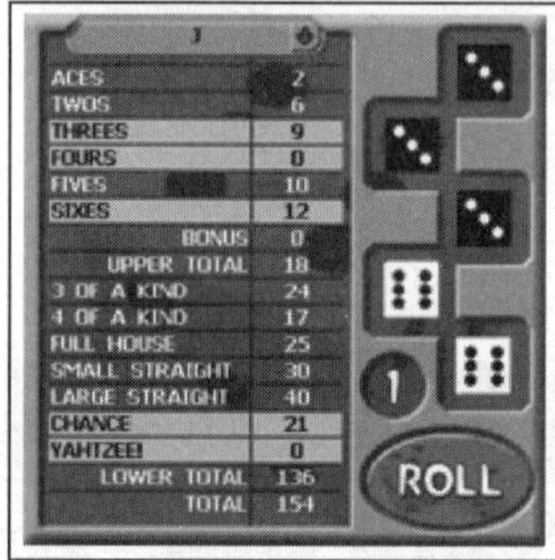

You can play any of these games solo (with one or more computer opponents, depending on the game) or with other people. In fact, all three games support play via infrared, meaning if you have, say, Battleship on your PDA and you're sitting across from someone who has Battleship on his PDA, you can play head-to-head on your respective devices. After you complete your turn, you tap a button to beam your move to the other person, where it's reflected on his screen. He makes his move, beams it to you, and so the game progresses. Of course, you can also take turns on the same PDA—it's just not as cool and geeky.

Killer Tip *These three games are great diversions for kids old enough to understand the rules. Each one requires at least a little bit of brain power (Scrabble in particular), as opposed to the usual blast-everything-in-sight games kids usually play. And because they're fun for adults as well, they're ideal for the whole family. This message brought to you by Parker Brothers. (Just kidding.)*

FIND IT ON THE CD

Battleship, $19.99
Scrabble, $29.99
Yahtzee, $19.99
Handmark
www.handmark.com

37 All Mobile Casino

Get Ready for Vegas, Baby

Hey, is that a casino in your pocket? It is if you're carrying Casino in your pocket. This collection of five gambling games includes blackjack, craps, poker, roulette, and slots—and we guarantee you'll never lose more than $17. Let's see Caesar's Palace match that bet!

Speaking of Vegas, there's nothing like a little blackjack practice before you hit the tables. Casino's version is quite nice, allowing you to play with anywhere from one to six decks (ideal for practicing your card counting), double down, get insurance, and so on. (Tap the Prefs button to change the various game settings.) Your bet stays the same for each hand unless you tap Menu | Table Bet, which gives you choices for different dollar amounts.

The other star of the Casino show is Nevada Craps, a sophisticated simulation that allows you to place almost every kind of bet available at the real tables. You can play solo or against up to three computer-controlled players.

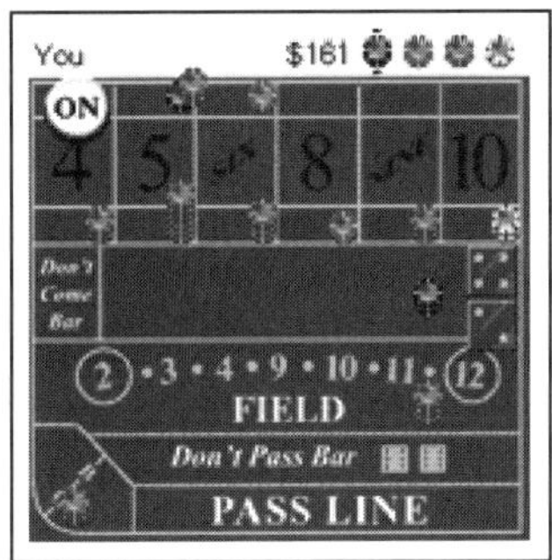

Roulette and slots offer the same kind of random fun as their real-world counterparts. Poker is the collection's only real disappointment—it's just video poker, meaning you get five cards dealt, keep the ones that look promising, and get a new deal for the rest. Pretty dull, if you ask us. If you're looking for a more robust poker game, Stand Alone sells one separately: Hold 'Em for Palm OS. This is a robust version of the popular Texas Hold 'Em game. Check out the demo on the CD!

Killer Tip *Not up to speed on the finer points of roulette or craps? Both games, as well as the three others, include detailed built-in instructions. Tap Menu | Rules (or Help if you're playing craps) to read them.*

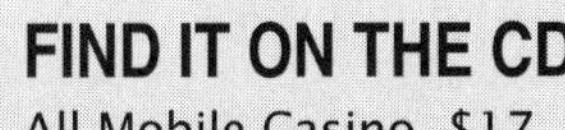

FIND IT ON THE CD

All Mobile Casino, $17
Stand Alone
www.standalone.com

38 ChessGenius

Hone Your Chess Skills

Whether you're serious about chess or you just enjoy the occasional casual game, there's no better Palm OS simulation than ChessGenius. The game caters to novices and experts alike and includes 40 different play levels. You can play solo against the computer, play against another person (either on the same PDA or via infrared, assuming your opponent also has ChessGenius installed on his or her PDA), or sit back and watch the computer play itself.

If you're an utter novice like Rick, you'll appreciate ChessGenius's ten beginner levels, in which the game makes deliberate mistakes. It can offer hints regarding your next move and, in Tutor mode, warn you if you've made a bad move. You can even "take it back" and try to make a better move. Once your skills improve, you can switch to the "blitz" levels—timed games in which you have anywhere from 1 minute to 120 minutes to play the entire match.

Killer Tip *Keep to the center of the board. Occupy it if you can, attack it if your opponent has it. Pawns make excellent soldiers in the war for the center.*

In short, ChessGenius has just about every feature you could want in a chess game, and then some. On the other hand, if you've always found chess a bit dull or slow-moving, have we got an alternative for you. Rook's Revenge (www.astraware.com) presents you with a colorful, but fairly traditional-looking, chess board. Instead of making moves one at a time, your goal is to make them as quickly as possible. You're still limited to the legal moves of each piece, but you don't have to wait for your opponent to make a move before you make your next one. It's like chess on steroids—terrific, addicting, fast-paced fun. Check out the demo on the CD!

FIND IT ON THE CD

ChessGenius, $25
Lang Software
www.chessgenius.com

39 Backgammon Pro

Ever Wonder Why There's No Frontgammon?

We love backgammon. It's like checkers for grown-ups. Stand Alone's Backgammon Pro offers just about everything you could want in a PDA version of the game, including one- and two-player competition, infrared play, whip-smart A.I. that learns from previous games, and even a choice of boards (we like the high-resolution "leather" one best).

While the gameplay options can be intimidating to those who play backgammon only casually, Stand Alone supplies an extensive illustrated manual (in HTML format, so fire up your web browser) that discusses settings and strategies. Indeed, Backgammon Pro is for those who want to master backgammon, not just enjoy the occasional informal game (though it's fine for that purpose). There's even a "visitor" mode so others can play without interfering with your statistics.

BP has a few small quirks, such as "white" pieces that are actually brown when you play on the aforementioned leather board. Plus, the interface could use a little polish. But don't let those minor complaints stop you from enjoying this backgammon powerhouse.

FIND IT ON THE CD
Backgammon Pro, $15
Stand Alone
www.standalone.com

40 Billiards

Shoot Some Stick

You don't have to be a big fan of pool to enjoy Billiards, one of the most visually dazzling Palm OS games we've ever seen. In fact, we'd say it's a must-have for anyone who owns a Palm Tungsten T3, Garmin iQue 3600, Sony Clié NR/NX/NZ/UX, or any other model with an oversize screen. Billiards shows off that screen like few other games (see Figure 4-2). (Fear not: it looks great on standard-size screens, too—just not quite as impressive.)

Billiards plays a mean game of pool, too. It's designed for one or two players and offers a variety of games (including Billiards, Pyramid, 9-ball, and three varieties of 8-ball). And according to Dave "Fats" Johnson (a nickname that, alas, has more to do with pant size than pool skill), the ball physics are spot-on. Rick "Cue Ball" Broida concurs.

Killer Tip *When the time comes to install Billiards, you'll discover that the Zip file contains a whopping ten different PRC files. Each one supports a different screen size or resolution or PDA model. Billiards-256Color.prc, for instance, is for models like the Palm IIIc, while Billiards-65K.prc would be your choice for the Handspring Visor Prism (which supports 65,000 colors, hence the "65K" designation). If you have one of the high-end Sony Clié models with a big screen, install Billiards-Sony-HRPlus-65K.prc. Need more help? Consult the Read_me_first!!!.txt file contained in the Zip file. It tells you exactly which PRC to install depending on your PDA model.*

Playing Billiards can be a little confusing at first until you understand the controls. First, tap and hold your stylus on the screen somewhere below the ball, then drag it

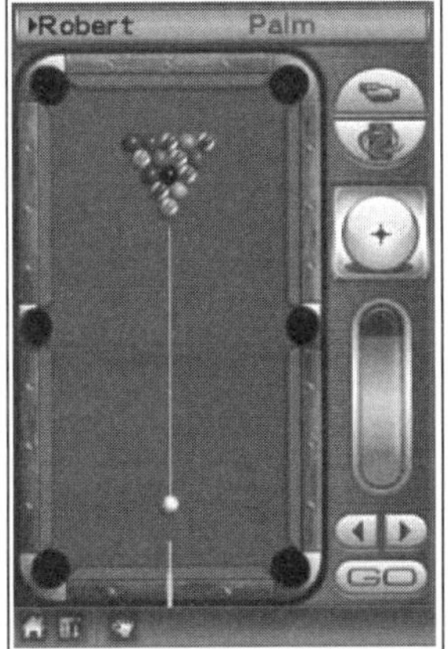

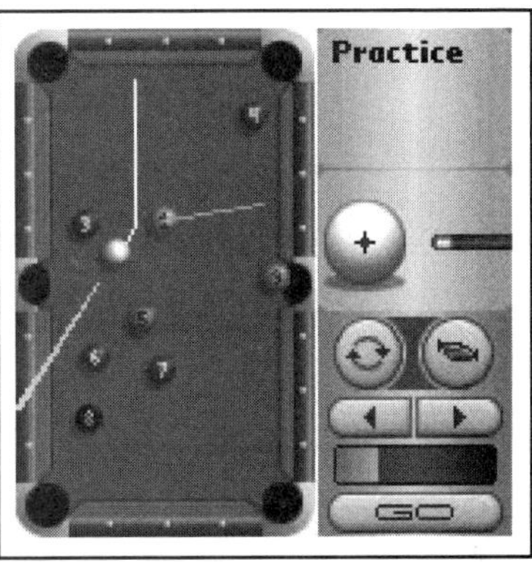

FIGURE 4-2 The "HiRes+" version of Billiards (left) takes full advantage of 320×480-pixel screens. But even the 320×320 version (right) looks gorgeous.

left and right. You'll see the cue stick move accordingly. This is how you line up your shot. If you have the Trace option enabled (tap Menu | Game | Options, then select it from the Tips & Tricks menu), you'll also see where the cue ball will strike the other balls. Using the controls on the right side of the screen, you can adjust the power of your shot, add spin to the ball, adjust the stick's angle of elevation, and so on.

Megasoft 2000 includes an excellent instruction manual in the Billiards Zip file. After you extract everything from it, find and open Manual.html and the instructions will appear in your web browser. Rack 'em up!

FIND IT ON THE CD
Billiards, $22.95
Megasoft2000
www.megasoft2000.com

41 Text Twist

A Game That Boggles the Mind

If you look at the letters GEVAAS and immediately see "savage," you're sure to enjoy Text Twist, an elegant variation on Boggle and one of Rick's all-time favorite games. The premise is simple: you're given six scrambled letters and two minutes in which to build as many words as possible. To score the maximum number of points and move on to the next level, you have to unscramble the six-letter word.

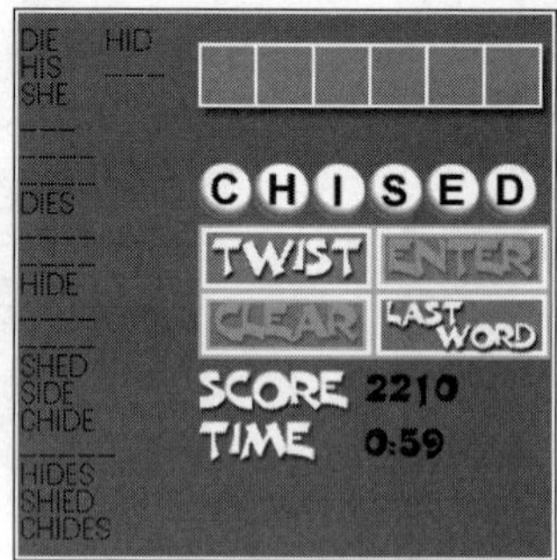

Text Twist has over 10,000 words in its dictionary, so you're not likely to run out anytime soon. If you get stuck while trying to build your words, you can tap the Twist button to reshuffle the letters. If you're really good, you'll get all the possible words before time runs out, and earn bonus points (and bragging rights) in the process.

Killer Tip *Astraware is responsible for some of the most popular PDA games on the planet. Ever heard of Bejeweled? The PDA version comes from Astraware. We also highly recommend BookWorm, Bounce Out, Insaniquarium, and especially Word Mojo, which is like Scrabble with a twist. You can download demos of these and other excellent Astraware games from the company's web site.*

FIND IT ON THE CD

Text Twist, $14.95
Astraware
www.astraware.com

42 Aggression

What's Life Without a Little Risk?

If you've been looking for an excuse to buy a new PDA, one with a large, high-resolution screen, you've found it. Aggression, a dazzling clone of the classic boardgame Risk, takes full advantage of the extra space, providing a wide-screen gaming experience like few Palm OS titles we've seen before. Fortunately, it runs just as well on standard high-res—and even low-res—screens, though with a little less pizzazz.

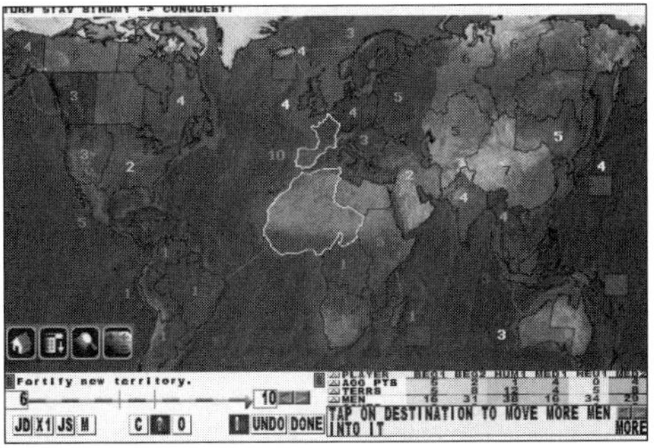

Like Risk, Aggression is a game of global domination. At the outset, you and up to five human and/or computer players divvy up the world's countries, then place your troops as strategically as possible. While there's strength in numbers, there's also the random element that comes from "rolling the dice" (which happens entirely behind the scenes, thus accelerating the game considerably). If you have eight troops and you're attacking a country with three, you're likely to capture it—but there's always the possibility you'll lose. Let the insanity begin.

Killer Tip *Even if you're familiar with Risk, you'll probably want to spend some time with Aggression's lengthy instruction manual, which is provided in HTML format and, therefore, must be opened in a web browser (you can print a copy from there, as well). While the game itself is quite easy to play, there are several gameplay options and interface items that aren't self-explanatory. Aggression does have a commendable built-in help system, but it doesn't go quite far enough.*

FIND IT ON THE CD

Aggression, $17.95
BLiT Games
www.blitgames.com

43 PDA Playground

Keep the Kids Entertained

As ideas go, PDA Playground can't be beat. It turns your handheld into a miniature game room, complete with six minigames and activities for kids aged three to seven. We've long been fans of this idea, as a PDA can be the perfect diversion for long car rides and other patience-draining situations. The software cleverly "locks out" all buttons and icons except Home and Menu, so there's no way your kids can accidentally erase data or switch to another program. In fact, you can add other third-party programs to PDA Playground's kid-friendly interface, so the little ones aren't limited to the software's six modules.

Speaking of which, PDA Playground's games are a mixed bag—but in a good way. Draw provides a paintbrush, color palette, eraser, fill tool, and spray paint, all for use on blank "paper." Paint (see Figure 4-3) sports the same tools, but offers 26 coloring-book pages with things like cats and teddy bears. ScratchOff requires kids to scribble all over the screen, thereby revealing one of the aforementioned pictures.

FIGURE 4-3 No crayons required for Paint, one of PDA Playground's six kid games. It lets your little one play with a digital coloring book.

FollowMe is a nice Simon-like memory game that uses animals, while PuzzlePath is a clever take on those old arrange-the-tiles games, except that here there's an animated little person you have to guide around a path. Finally, there's Match, a Concentration-style memory game we didn't think much of at first, but Rick's daughter Sarah has fun with it.

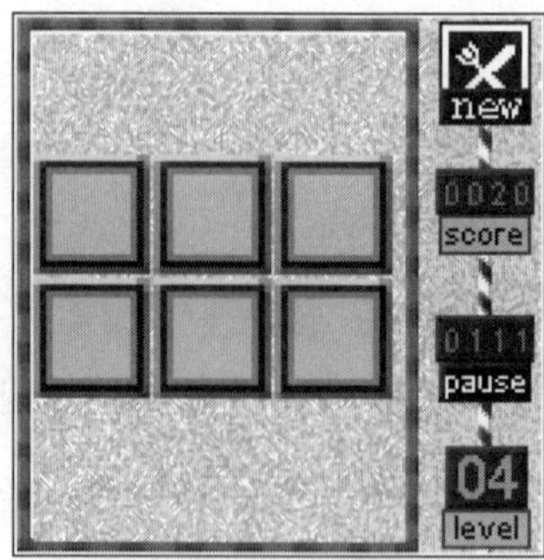

Killer Tip *Don't forget that to get out of PDA Playground, or even to HotSync your PDA, you must first exit the program. If one of the modules is running, tap Home, then Menu | Leave PDA Playground. If you're already at the main screen, do just the latter step.*

FIND IT ON THE CD

PDA Playground, $19.95
DataViz
www.dataviz.com

Chapter 5

Built-In Apps Done Better

Your Palm is packed with a great collection of PIM programs. You know—Personal Information Manager stuff. Your calendar, contacts, to do lists, and notes. They're all in there. After all, that's probably why you bought your PDA to begin with. And then there's Graffiti, the program that lets you input data into your Palm via handwriting recognition. It's not hard to learn, and is mighty convenient.

But those built-in apps aren't perfect. The Date Book is an easy way to share your calendar with your desktop PC, but it's far from the most powerful tool around for managing your schedule. Graffiti, moreover, doesn't agree with everyone that tries to learn it. With just a little sleuthing, you can find some truly excellent replacements for those programs. The right replacements can make your day a little easier; they can make your Palm a little more fun. We've rounded up the best of the best in built-in app substitutes and offered them for you here in this chapter. After adding programs like Contacts 5, simpliWrite, and TapPad, you'll wonder how you ever got by with your unmodified Palm.

44 Contacts 5

Turbocharge the Address Book

POWER APP

Forget about the anemic Address Book built into your Palm. Contacts 5, from PDA Performance, is a high-powered replacement that packs so many cool features into a single program that you'll never go back to the plain Palm software again.

Here's the program in a snapshot:

After installing it, you can start using it right away; it automatically reads the same contact data that was in the Address Book. In fact, the Address Book is still on your Palm, and you can use it if you prefer, even with Contacts 5 installed.

The program has many preferences, modes, and features. Some of the highlights:

- In List View (the program default), you can open a contact by tapping on the name. Tap on the phone number, though, and you see a pop-up menu to switch the displayed phone number to another option or to dial the number immediately—if you have a smartphone or the ability to dial a phone using a feature like Bluetooth.

- Switch to SmartContacts View by tapping on the icon second from the right:

In this mode, you can enable Finger Search to find a contact by tapping on the number pad until you spell any part of the name or company. It's a fast way to zero in on a specific entry.

- The program is chock-full of tabs and buttons. You can add a new entry, beam contacts, or access program options from the first three buttons at the bottom of the screen. And once you are looking at a specific entry, notice the tabs that help organize the various bits of data you can associate with each person or company:

FIND IT ON THE CD
Contacts 5, $19.95
PDA Performance
www.pdaperformance.com

45 Agendus

Turbocharge the Date Book

Seemingly named after one of the lesser Roman gods, Agendus is actually the new name for a program that old hands from the PDA's earlier days may recall: Action Names. But don't let the name change throw you; Agendus is one of the best Date Book replacements for the Palm OS. The only other program that's even in the same league with Agendus is a program called DateBk 5, which offers many of the same features and also is famous for its not-for-profit status. All proceeds from DateBk 5 go toward Dewar's www.gorilla-haven.org Gorilla Haven project in the North Georgia Mountains. You can learn more about DateBk 5 at www.pimlicosoftware.com.

Agendus seamlessly combines your Address Book, Date Book, and To Do List into a single, powerful program. Its power is impressive. You can link To Dos and Date Book appointments to entries in your Address Book, effortlessly maintain a contact history with clients, apply color icons to your calendar events, and see your daily activities on a split screen with your To Dos. If you have a 320×480-pixel device like a Sony Clié or

Palm Tungsten T3, Agendus will take full advantage of the larger display, as you can see here:

When you first start the program, you'll find a Today View (similar to the Palm's startup screen), which you can "wallpaper" with a favorite digital image from your PDA's memory card. To do that, your image needs to be in the GIF format; JPG images won't work. The easiest way to load wallpaper is to copy your GIF to your Palm's memory card and then choose Options | Preferences from the menu. Select Wallpaper from the Category menu at the top of the screen. Then find the file and click OK.

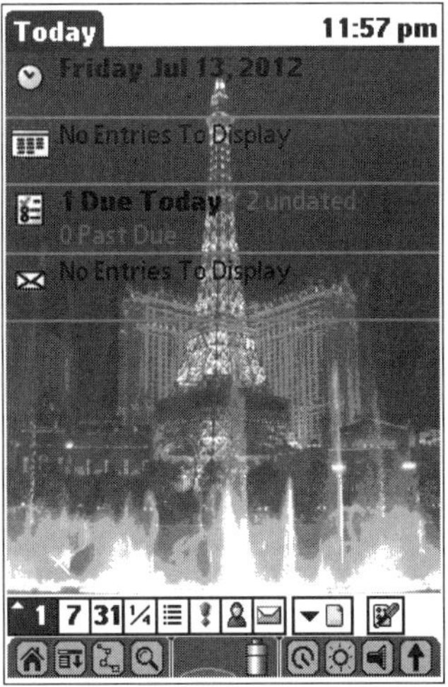

Note that you can link an appointment to a contact very easily. Open a meeting, and you can enter a contact at the top of the screen.

After you click OK, it's easy to open the contact from the Meeting screen or see meetings from the contact page. (To do that, find the entry in the contact page and tap and hold. From the drop-down menu, choose Contact History.)

FIND IT ON THE CD

Agendus, $24.95
iambic
www.iambic.com

46 ToDo PLUS

Turbocharge the To Do List

Do you use your Palm's To Do List? Probably not. And that's too bad, because it's a really useful tool for keeping track of, well, things you need to do. The problem with the Palm's built-in To Do List is that it's too anemic, though. That's why we recommend that you pop a copy of ToDo PLUS onto your PDA.

What's so cool about it? Check out this image of the program:

The icons at the bottom of the screen give you a slew of capabilities right at your fingertips without ever entering the menus. To create a new to do, tap the Clipboard. Write your message. From there, you can

- Tap the Note icon to add a free-form note with more information.
- Tap the Drawing icon to attach a sketch to the to do. That's right—you can draw a picture to help you rapidly store important information.

- Alarm the to do. It's true—if you want to add an alarm to an event, you can always put it in the Date Book, but the Palm's standard To Do List doesn't ring alarms at all. But having the ability to alarm to dos gives you a lot of extra flexibility. Want to write "get milk" and alarm it for the end of the day? You can do it here.

Finally, be sure to check out the filters in the drop-down menu at the top left of the screen. There are a lot of ways to see your to dos—great if you have a lot of them. Our favorite: the Radar option, which shows all tasks that are either overdue, have no due date, or are due within seven days. With ToDo PLUS, you'll never miss an important task again.

FIND IT ON THE CD
ToDo PLUS, $19.95
Hands High Software
www.handshigh.com

47 Memo PLUS

Turbocharge the Memo Pad

We've got a treat for you. If you thought that ToDo PLUS was cool, you're going to totally flip for Memo PLUS.

Okay, maybe that's a bit melodramatic. We're geeks. We love stuff like this. But even if you're not quite as passionate as, say, Rick when he discovers a new font for his Palm, we think you're going to be jazzed about this.

Memo PLUS, like ToDo PLUS, is a replacement for the built-in app from Hands High Software. Like ToDo PLUS, Memo PLUS gives you a slew of new buttons at the bottom of the screen for using memos quickly and easily:

To create a new note, tap the first icon on the left. Once in the memo editor, you can add an alarm or a hand-drawn sketch from the icons at the bottom of the screen.

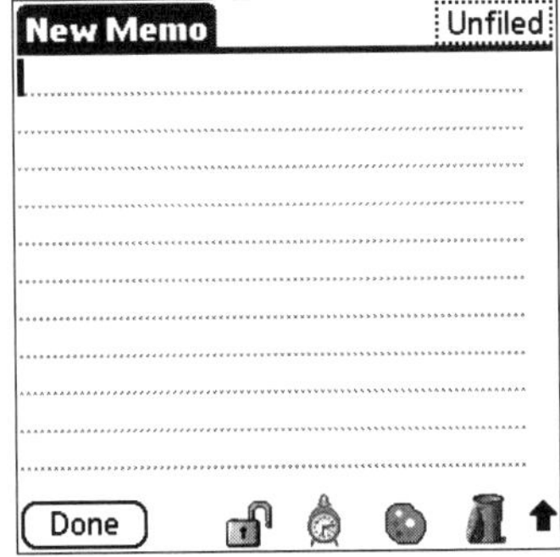

In addition to just creating memos, Memo PLUS also lets you create drawings that aren't attached to any particular memo; these appear in the memo list. To make such a sketch, tap the Drawing button when you're on the main screen.

The coolest feature in Memo PLUS is the ability to use templates. If you want to create a standard memo that you can make changes to as needed, then templates are for you. Suppose, for instance, that you are a spy conducting surveillance on a highway, and you need to quickly write down the color and make of passing cars. You might want a template that looks like this:

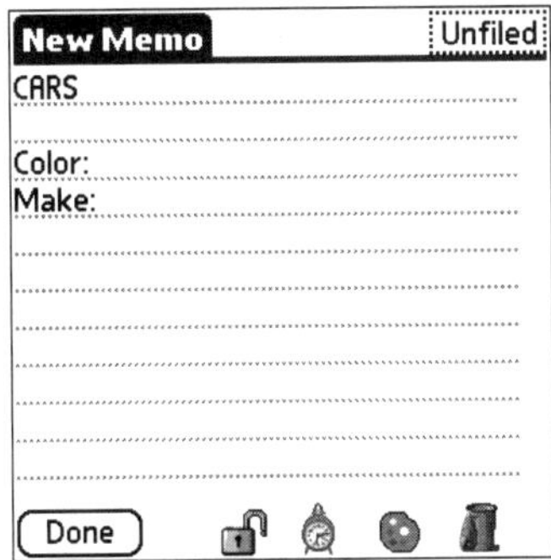

When you see a car, you can create a new memo based on a template, fill in the blanks, and save the memo so you're ready to create a new memo when the next car passes. Do this:

1. Choose Note | Edit Note Tmpls from the menu.
2. Tap New to create a new template.
3. Create the text that you want to appear in the memo every time you open a new note based on this template.

4. Tap Done, then tap OK to close the template editor.
5. Now it's time to open a new memo from a template. Tap the arrow to the right of the new memo button. Choose the template you created and tap OK. Make the changes to your memo and tap Done.

Killer Tip *The lightning bolt on the right side of the screen is a quick-launch button. You can add any programs on the Palm to this list and then launch your favorite apps with a single tap from Memo PLUS.*

FIND IT ON THE CD
Memo PLUS, $19.95
Hands High Software
www.handshigh.com

48 simpliWrite

Easier Handwriting Recognition

If you have a Palm, you probably know Graffiti pretty well. But it's not always the best way to get data into your PDA. And if you have an older Palm—one that runs a version of the operating system prior to OS 5, you might be jealous of the new enhanced handwriting recognition, Graffiti 2. Graffiti 2 allows you to write anywhere on the screen—you're not required to write in the small Graffiti area at the bottom of the display. And Graffiti 2 makes certain letters easier to draw thanks to more logical strokes. A *t*, for instance, is one stroke down and one across, instead of the traditional Graffiti one-stroke method, as you can see here:

A program called simpliWrite, from Advanced Recognition Technologies, can turn your older Palm into something that works a lot like a new Graffiti 2 model. When you install the program, you simply need to enable it on this screen:

From there, you'll see the simpliWrite icon at the bottom of the screen, telling you it's okay to write with SimpliWrite gestures. Available at any time from the help screen, here's a snapshot of the most common simpliWrite letters and numbers:

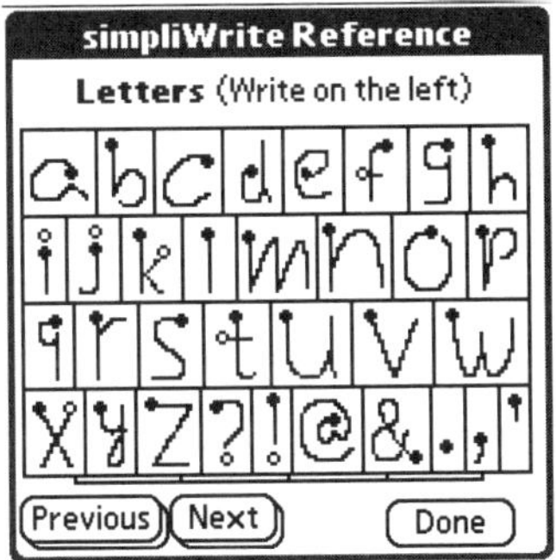

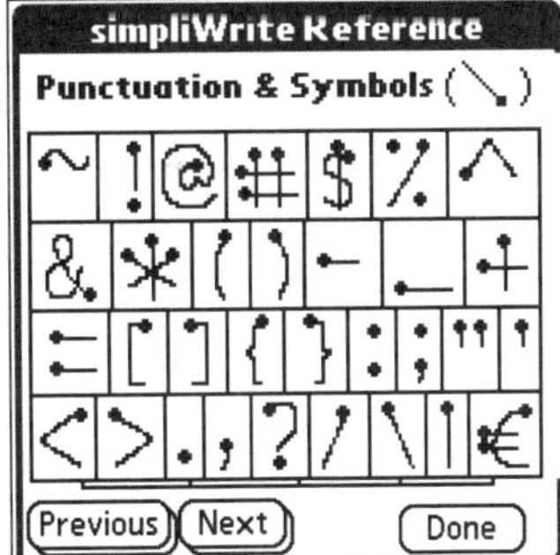

Killer Tip *No matter what version of Graffiti you have, you can see a tip sheet of the most important Graffiti gestures by drawing a line from the bottom of the screen to the top. Handy for reminding yourself how to make that pesky letter Q.*

FIND IT ON THE CD

simpliWrite, $19.95
Advanced Recognition Technologies
www.simpliwrite.com

49 MiddleCaps

Easier Capital Letters

Some apps are cool; others are useful. This one—if you don't have a new Graffiti 2-style Palm OS device—is absolutely essential.

Consider the problem. With Graffiti, the only way to write capital letters is to perform an upstroke first, which sets the device into CAPS mode. If you want to write in ALL CAPS, you need to make not one but two upstrokes. That's not hard, but it's certainly counterintuitive. And you'll forget to do it occasionally and have to erase and rewrite a bunch of text.

MiddleCaps avoids that problem by letting you specify a region in the Graffiti area that automatically sets text to CAPS. Most users make this the division between letters and numbers.

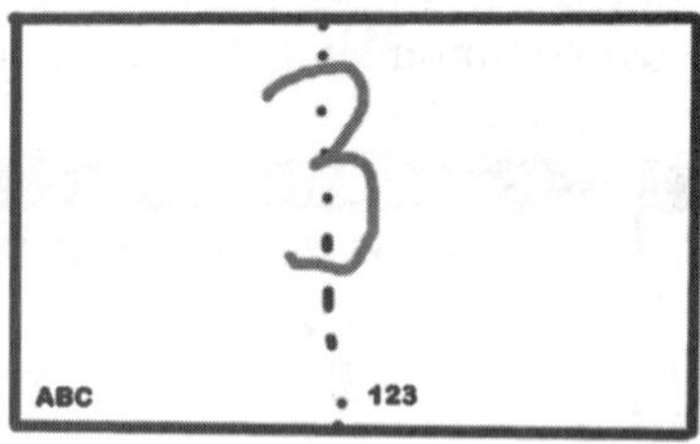

In order to use MiddleCaps, you need a Palm device that runs OS 4 or lower—it will not work with OS 5 or higher. That's because MiddleCaps requires a hack manager—a program like Hackmaster or X-Master, which only runs on Palms with OS 4 or lower.

Hacks are utilities that modify the operation of the Palm OS. Despite the name, Hacks are not dangerous or unstable. A community of developers has created dozens of useful Hacks like MiddleCaps for the Palm OS. Hacks don't work by themselves, though. You need X-Master or Hackmaster to "manage" the hacks. Installing these two programs is really trivial, though, and we think you'll agree that it's well worth the effort.

MiddleCaps, Free
Rui Oliveria
www.palmgear.com

50 Keyboard Hack II

A Better Built-In Keyboard

Hopefully you already know that you're not forced to use the Graffiti writing area for all of your text-input needs. If you are entering a password, for instance, or some other data that requires precise entry and you don't want to mess with Graffiti, just switch to the built-in keyboard. To do that, just tap on the abc or the 123 in the bottom corners of the Graffiti area. If you tap on abc, you'll get a keyboard that looks like this:

Tap the 123, and you'll see this instead:

And no matter which keyboard you start with, you can easily switch between them by tapping the abc, 123, and Int'l buttons at the bottom of the keyboard. When you're done entering data, just tap the Done button.

Killer Tip *The keyboard will only appear if you are using a program that accepts text entry. If not, tapping the abc or 123 will just generate a system "beep."*

All that is well and good, but the fact remains that the built-in keyboard leaves a lot to be desired. The keyboard is laid out like a QWERTY keyboard, but it's incomplete—the numbers and special characters are on a separate screen.

Keyboard Hack II, on the other hand, gives you all those things in a simple, inexpensive package. It works in conjunction with a hack manager like Hackmaster or X-Master. Here is a look at what Keyboard Hack II looks like in operation:

Killer Tip *If you try the OS 5 version of Keyboard Hack II, keep in mind that there's no need for a hack manager like X-Master. It runs without a hack manager, which wouldn't work in OS 5 anyway.*

FIND IT ON THE CD
Keyboard Hack II, $8.95
PalmGadget
www.palmgadget.com

51 TapPad

Give Graffiti a Helping Hand

It's probably starting to sound like we're doing nothing but ragging on Graffiti. We don't like making capital letters. We want to write anywhere on the screen. We don't like the built-in keyboard. Well, despite our complaints, the honest truth is that Graffiti is pretty good, but we like to help it along from time to time. And to make matters worse, Rick just likes to complain.

Nonetheless, there's no better single program, we think, than TapPad for dramatically improving Graffiti. In fact, if TapPad looked a little less like software and a little more like Halle Berry, Dave would marry it.

TapPad is a program that changes the behavior of Graffiti by giving you one-tap access to special features while you enter data. The biggest change is that instead of writing numbers, TapPad divides the right side of the Graffiti area into a grid. Tap to enter numbers the same way you'd access numbers on a keyboard's number pad or on a calculator.

There are other buttons as well. Spanning the top of the alphabetic side of the Graffiti area, you have buttons for common features like cut, copy, paste, and delete.

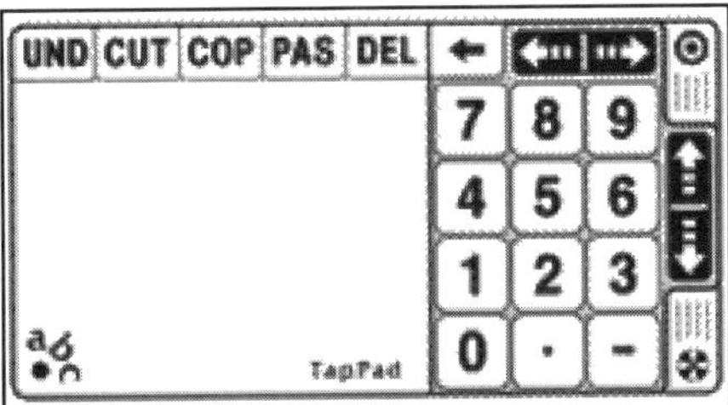

Sound good? It is. But, as you can probably guess, software alone isn't enough in most cases. After all—how do you know where to tap on the numeric side to get each number? That's where the overlays come in. When you buy TapPad, you get a set of adhesive, translucent screen-protector overlays. The overlays have the appropriate buttons marked, so you just tap on the overlay to access TapPad's features.

Killer Tip *To try the version of TapPad on the CD, you can print a paper overlay for testing purposes. It's included in the TapPad trial.*

If you have a Sony Clié NX70, you're in luck: there's a software-only version of TapPad that uses the virtual Graffiti area to display the TapPad overlay onscreen.

FIND IT ON THE CD
TapPad, $19.95
Brochu Software
www.tappad.com

52 PenJammer

And If You Can't Master Graffiti...

Okay, bear with us for one more Graffiti-related tip. Can't quite get the hang of your PDA's text input engine? Then try PenJammer.

PenJammer is a very complete tutorial for Graffiti that doesn't just teach you the letters and numbers; it has lessons for just about every possible gesture under the sun, including punctuation and special characters. That's great, because we have been using

Graffiti since the very first Palm Pilot came out in the 1990s and we still can't tell you how to draw a $, #, or &.

When you launch PenJammer, you get to choose whether to use it in Learn or Play Mode. In Learn Mode, you see exactly how each gesture is drawn with a slow animation, then you get to reproduce it. Do it well and you move on to the next character.

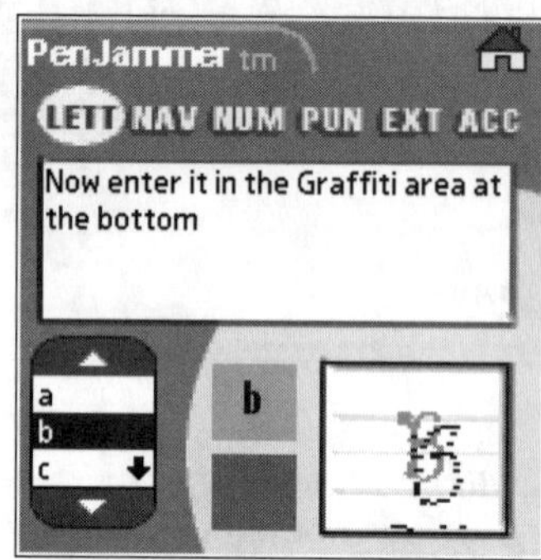

In Play Mode, you have to clear the screen of characters by drawing the correct gestures.

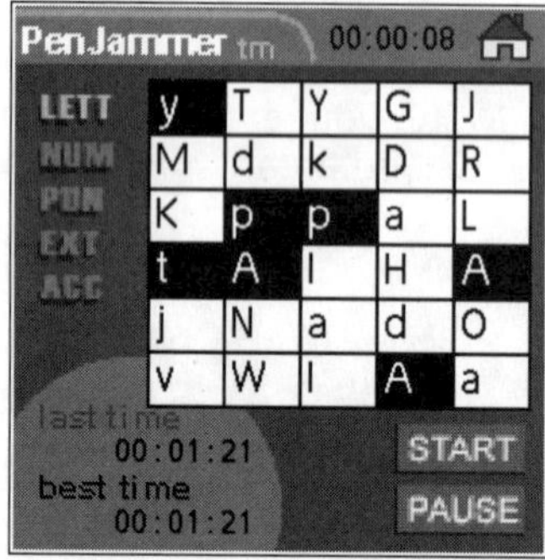

You may not need to keep this application on your Palm forever, but it'll certainly help you conquer Graffiti—and that's exactly the point.

FIND IT ON THE CD

PenJammer, $9.90
Ironwheel Works
www.penjammer.com

Share Calendars with Your Significant Other

Let's say that you're trying to coordinate your schedule with a friend, spouse, coworker, or parole officer. If your buddy is as busy as you are, how on Earth can you reconcile your schedules to meet for lunch or that parole hearing?

Try DualDate, a program offered for free from PalmOne. This program acts as an alternative to your built-in Date Book application and lets you show two calendars side-by-side on the same screen. Once installed on both PDAs, you can send your calendar to someone else by pointing your Palm infrared port at the other Palm OS device and choosing Record | Share Calendar from the menu.

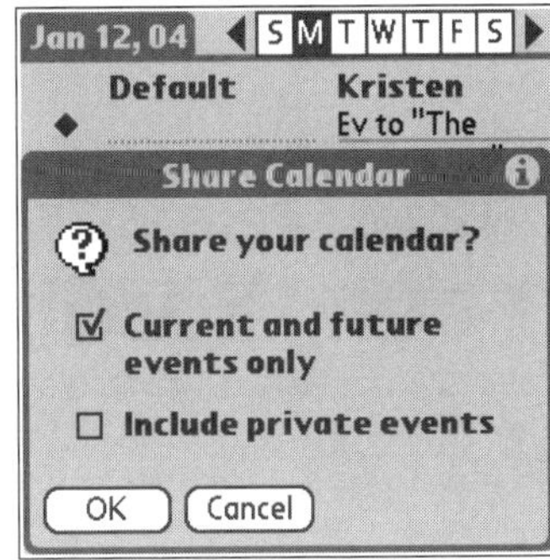

Your appointments will be sent to the other device and displayed in a second column, as you can see here:

To get your buddy's appointments, he or she will have to do the same and beam the other schedule to you. While the updates are not automatic—you have to manually beam updated calendars to each other on a regular basis to stay in sync—it's an easy way to keep someone else's appointments on your own PDA.

Killer Tip *If you want to keep your calendar in sync with a spouse, buddy, or coworker, try adding an appointment to the Date Book. When it pops up once a week or so, you'll remember it's time to match calendars with DualDate.*

FIND IT ON THE CD
DualDate, Free
PalmOne
www.palmone.com

54 WordComplete

Complete Your Words

Remember a few pages back when we said that we were done with Graffiti enhancements? Well, we lied. Here's one more for you—and this one will increase your text-entry speed even if you're a Graffiti expert and love using gestures to enter data into your Palm.

That's because WordComplete operates under the assumption that everyone would like to be able to enter less data while still getting all of their work done. So WordComplete is a word prediction system—it guesses what word you mean after you enter a few letters, and provides options for you to pick from a drop-down menu. Suppose you start writing a word on your Palm. You enter the letters *O* and *F*. Here are the options WordComplete gives you:

Off

Often

Office

If you enter a second *F*, the drop-down menu changes to these options:

Offer

Offered

Official

At any point, you can accept one of these words by tapping it or just keep entering letters and ignore the menu. That's the beauty of WordComplete: it helps without getting in the way. Here is what the program looks like when suggesting some words in Memo Pad:

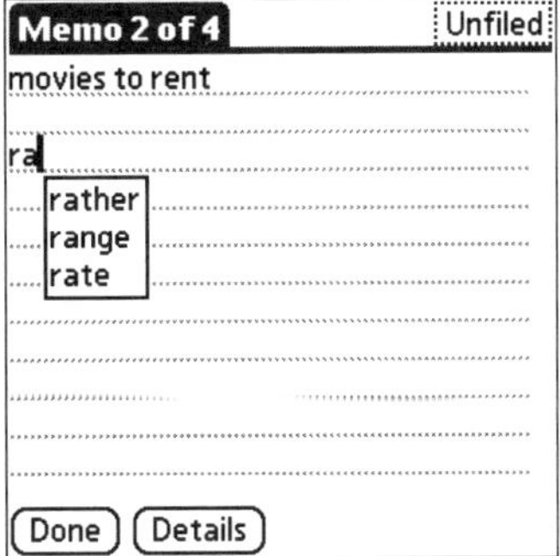

When you first install the program, be sure to turn it on; to do that, tap on the WordComplete icon and tap Enable WordComplete.

From there, you can fine-tune the way the program works. You can change the number of letters that WordComplete waits before suggesting a word, and how many words that the program displays in its suggestion list.

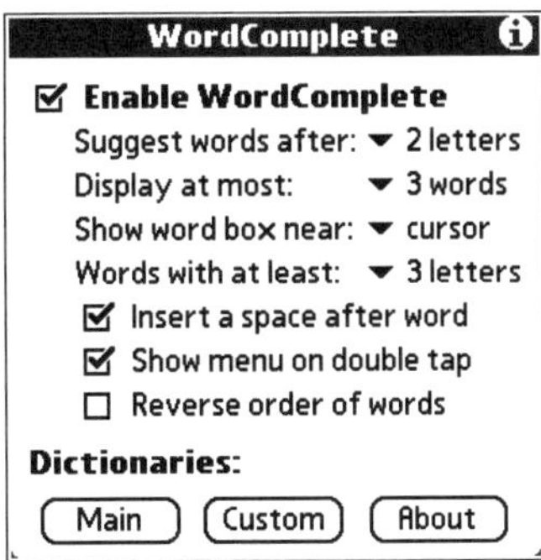

The built-in word dictionary has about 14,000 words. You can modify this word list, though. To add a new word to the dictionary, tap the Custom button at the bottom of the WordComplete screen. Write your new word and tap Add. Tap Close when you're done.

FIND IT ON THE CD
WordComplete, $24.99
Communication Intelligence Corporation
www.cic.com

55 SilverScreen

Launcher Madness

A lot of people get by with the Palm without ever realizing that it's possible to radically change the look and operation of the operating system. Big deal, you say—why would anyone want to? Because the standard Palm application launcher is kind of boring; it's not very attractive, and it's not easy to use. You have to run to the menu just to beam or delete a program, for instance, and there's no such thing as "drag and drop" in the world of Palm. Instead, you can install a launcher to get those kinds of features. It sounds like a small thing, but try a launcher just once and we predict you'll be bitten by the launcher bug.

There are at least a half dozen launchers out there to choose from. But in our quest to give you the very best, one program jumped out at us. SilverScreen takes the prize among launchers for one important feature: sheer beauty. SilverScreen was designed from the ground up to make your Palm-powered PDA look amazing. While most launchers simply pack the default application icons into whatever skin you've selected, SilverScreen renders beautifully customized icons instead. It's most noticeable when you have a high-resolution device, since the icons are noticeably sharper and more colorful than the default graphics.

Then there are the skins. SilverScreen has some of the most attractive skins in the business, and this is one of the few launchers that compel us to change the look of our device frequently. The holiday-inspired Xmas Eve theme, for instance, decks out all the app icons as tree ornaments, and the toolbar at the bottom of the screen becomes a festive snowy village. Finally, you can display GIF and JPG images in the launcher background for a custom wallpaper effect.

SilverScreen isn't all good looks, though. The program offers icon and text-based list views of your apps, tabbed categories, and drag-and-drop file activities. To beam a program to another Palm, for instance, just drag the icon onto the Beam button on the toolbar at the bottom of the screen. You can even assign special functions to several extra buttons at the bottom of the screen. We use those buttons to launch our favorite applications, but you can also use them to shut off the PDA, start Prefs, or perform any of another dozen tasks.

SilverScreen has other cool features. You can replace the toolbar with scrolling tickers that display date-sensitive data like appointments and to dos, or download tickers from PocketSensei that display TV listings, famous birthdays, sports schedules, and more.

FIND IT ON THE CD

SilverScreen, $19.95
PocketSensei
www.pocketsensei.com

Chapter 6

Learn Something

In case we haven't sufficiently driven home this point yet, your PDA is much more than just a pocket organizer—it's a pocket computer. And anything that smart riding around in your pocket should be able to teach you a thing or two. New vocabulary words, facts about France, dangerous drug interactions—that kind of thing. In this chapter, we look at software for students, teachers, and learners alike, as well as an indispensable tool for doctors and patients (hint: it has something to do with dangerous drug interactions).

56 LearnFlash

Festoon Your Vocabulary

Want to increase your word power? Sure, you can buy one of those word-a-day calendars, but they're awfully slow—only one word per day! A better option is LearnFlash, which helps build your vocabulary via multiple-choice quizzes. Once you register the program (which costs a mere $8), you gain access to all the databases at the developer's web site—and there are dozens devoted to vocabulary. You can also build your own database of terms, which is helpful if you're studying for a test or need to learn specific words.

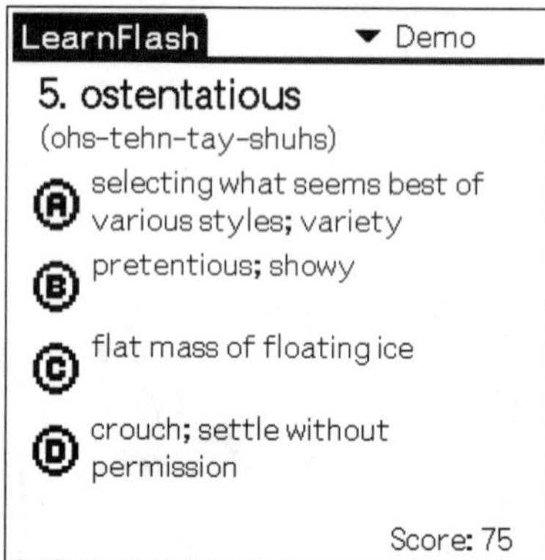

To get started building your vocabulary, install LearnFlash and at least one Vocab database (you can find them by clicking the site's Downloads link). When you first run the program, you have to select a database you want to use. Tap the arrow at the top of the screen next to Personal, then tap the name of the database you installed. Your quiz will begin, with LearnFlash keeping a running tally of your score as you progress.

Killer Tip *None of the LearnFlash database files is zipped, meaning that after you download one, you can double-click it to have it added directly to the Palm Install Tool for your next HotSync.*

To build your own database of terms, tap Menu | Options | Data Manager, and then tap New to start your list. Now enter the word, its phonetic (if you need it), and its definition. Wash, rinse, repeat.

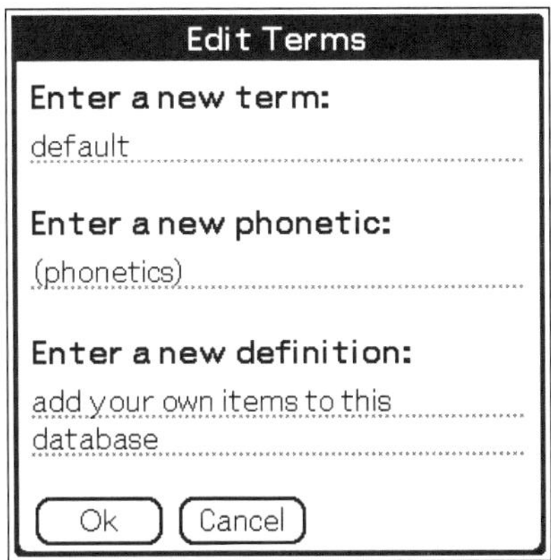

The LearnFlash site is home to more than just general vocabulary databases. You can also learn stock-market and trading terms, wine-tasting and related terms, and sushi and related terms (no, we're not making that up).

FIND IT ON THE CD
LearnFlash, $8
Bart Pinto
http://learnflash.virtualave.net

57 WordSleuth Thesaurus

What's Another Word for Thesaurus?

For students, writers, and other folks who rely heavily on language, nothing beats a good thesaurus. Unfortunately, a good thesaurus usually weighs a couple pounds and nabs more than its fair share of a backpack or bookcase. WordSleuth Thesaurus puts a whopping 210,000 synonyms in your pocket, yet weighs zero pounds, zero ounces. Take that, Roget!

Though it's not the only thesaurus available for the Palm OS, there are two things we particularly like about WordSleuth. First, despite its extensive word library, it requires only 200KB of memory on your PDA. Second, it couldn't be easier to use. Just write in the word you want to look up (or paste it in from another application, as described in the next paragraph), tap the Lookup button, and you're done. You can narrow down the search results by tapping the tabs on the right side of the screen, which organize the synonyms by parts of speech.

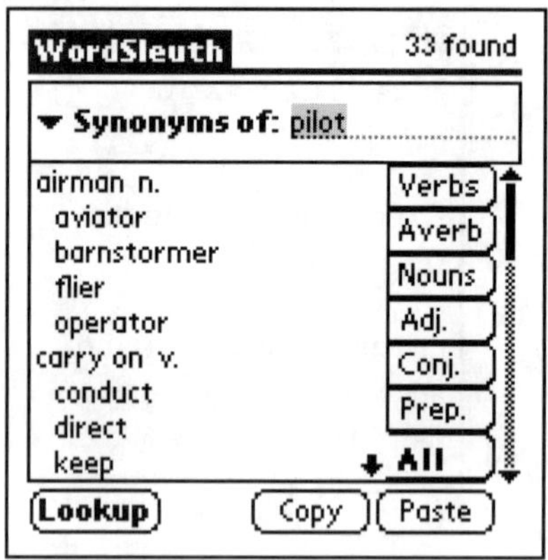

WordSleuth includes bidirectional copy and paste features. Let's say you're working in Memo Pad and need another word for, say, *memo*. Double-tap the word to highlight it, then tap Menu | Edit | Copy. (You can also write the Graffiti shortcut stroke followed by a **C**.) Exit Memo Pad, run WordSleuth, and tap the Paste button. You'll see the word *memo* appear automatically in the lookup field. When you find a suitable substitute, tap it, tap Copy, and then return to Memo Pad. Now tap Menu | Edit | Paste, and presto: there's your synonym.

Killer Tip *If you discover that you use WordSleuth quite a bit, you can save a lot of time by reassigning one of your PDA's buttons to launch it. To do so, return to the Home screen, tap the Prefs icon, then navigate to the Buttons menu. Choose the button you want to reassign, then select WordSleuth from the list of choices. Better yet, install a utility that lets you launch more than one program from each button. We recommend 1 Button Launcher (available for $10 from www.palmgear.com).*

If you have RAM to spare and want a thesaurus that's a bit more sophisticated, check out the PocketLingo Thesaurus (www.pocketlingo.com). Based on *Roget's II The New Thesaurus, Third Edition,* it ups the ante to 244,000 synonyms and includes MyWord and Study Card features for words you want to learn and review. However, it nabs just over 2MB of storage space—ten times as much as WordSleuth. Fortunately, you can install it to and run it from a memory card.

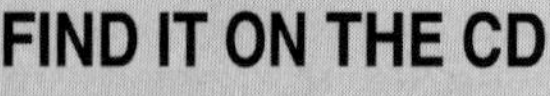

FIND IT ON THE CD

WordSleuth Thesaurus, $14.95
LandWare
www.landware.com

Keep Track of School Assignments

For students in high school or college, organization is half the battle. There's so much information to keep track of—assignments, test dates, instructor info, class locations, grades, and so on—that it can interfere with a successful academic career. Enter 4.0Student, which stores all that information and more for fast and easy reference. It can even add coursework reminders to your appointment calendar and to do list.

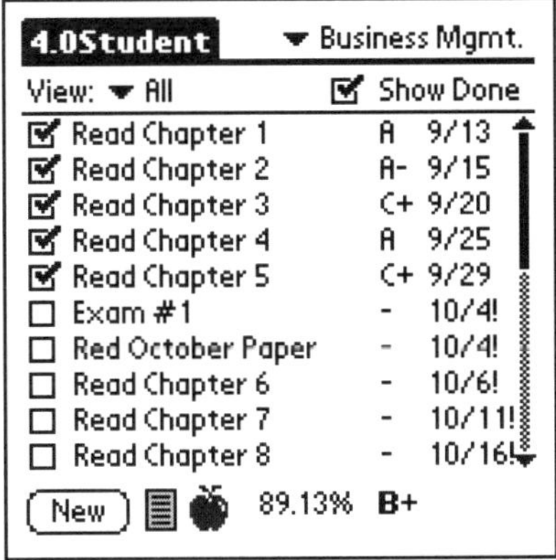

4.0Student can seem a little intimidating at first, if only because you start with an almost entirely blank screen. Here's the step-by-step procedure for getting started:

1. Tap Menu | Class | New, then enter all the pertinent details regarding your class (name, time, days, a web page if applicable, and so on). Tap OK when you're done.
2. If you want to add information about the instructor, tap the apple icon at the bottom of the screen, then record items like office hours, phone number, and e-mail address.
3. Add your first assignment, test, or other kind of coursework by tapping Menu | Class | Add Coursework. Here you can enter the due date, the corresponding textbook (only one, unfortunately), and your final score once the item has been graded. Notice, too, the options to add the coursework to your PDA's

datebook or to do list. Just tap the corresponding button once you've filled in the name and due date, and 4.0Student will copy the data to the proper program.

4. If your instructor or school has a specific grading policy, tap Menu | Class | Grading Policy to adjust percentages and how they translate to letter grades.

Entering all this information on your PDA can be awkward and time-consuming. 4.0Student doesn't come with a desktop component for synchronization, but there is another option. It's called Fourostudent.net (see Figure 6-1), a Web-based service where you can type in all your class and coursework on your PC, then synchronize it with 4.0Student on your PDA. The service also enables you to print copies of your records and even share them online with teachers and other students. A one-year subscription to Fourostudent.net adds $10 to the price of 4.0Student; a two-year subscription adds $20.

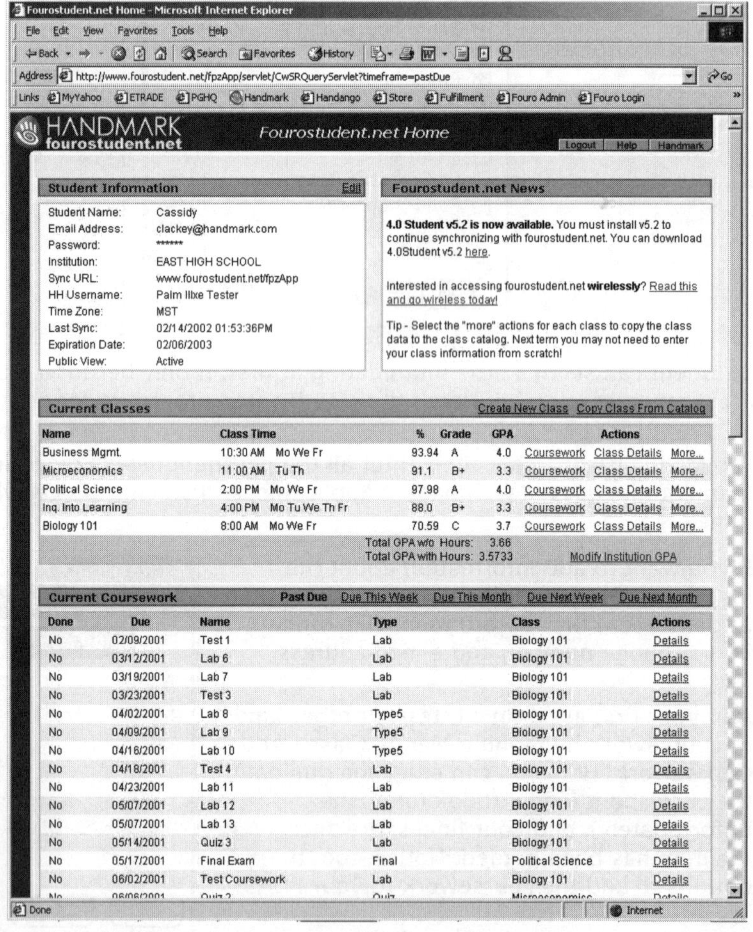

FIGURE 6-1 With an optional subscription to Fourostudent.net, you can synchronize your 4.0Student data with the Web—and enter new data much more easily.

Killer Tip *Not sure if you can pull up your GPA by the end of the year? Use 4.0Student's What If feature to calculate how remaining tests and assignments will affect your final grade. Tap Menu | Options | What If, and then plug in the grades you expect to get. Before you can do this, however, you have to enter all the upcoming coursework in 4.0Student's main screen.*

FIND IT ON THE CD
4.0Student, $19.99
Handmark
www.handmark.com

59 ePocrates Rx

A Drug Database for Doctors and Patients

If you're a doctor, healthcare worker, or someone who takes a lot of medication, you need to know about ePocrates Rx. One of the all-time great PDA freebies, ePocrates Rx is a regularly updated drug database that includes extensive information on over 2,800 drugs—everything from adult and pediatric doses to contraindications, drug interactions, and adverse reactions. The latest version also includes formulary information from a wide variety of hospitals and health plans, so you can see which drugs are covered and even search for preferred therapeutic alternatives. Finally, there's a Multicheck feature that lets you look up potentially harmful interactions between two or more drugs. Needless to say, whether you're the one prescribing the medication or the one taking it, this kind of information could prove invaluable.

As with programs like AvantGo (see Chapter 9) and Vindigo (see Chapter 2), ePocrates Rx downloads updates via your PC's Internet connection. Thus, if you use America Online or some other dial-up service, make sure you're signed on before you HotSync.

Killer Tip *Synchronizing with the ePocrates servers can add a couple extra minutes to the HotSync process. If you've already done a HotSync the same day and don't want to wait, just tap Cancel when the ePocrates status box appears. Your PDA will simply skip the connection during this HotSync. No data will be lost.*

As wonderful as the free version of ePocrates is, ePocrates Rx Pro is even better. The $59.99 annual subscription fee includes clinical tables, treatment guidelines, and data on alternative medicines and their interactions with prescription drugs. The Pro version also includes an infectious-diseases guide, a medical calculator (which computes things like ideal body weight and mean arterial pressure), and DocAlerts—clinical news from the FDA, CIC, and other organizations (some of them commercial in nature).

Because the software requires a subscription to the ePocrates service, we couldn't include it on the CD. There is, however, a link to the company's web site, where you can download the program.

FIND IT ON THE CD
ePocrates Rx Clinical Drug Database, Free
ePocrates, Inc.
www.epocrates.com

60 The 2004 World Almanac, Handheld Edition Bundle

A Knack for Almanacs

If ever a program made a case for converting printed reference works into electronic books, it's Town Compass's The 2004 World Almanac. Forget for a moment the obvious advantage: one less heavy, bulky book to carry around. The real benefit here is the speed with which you can find what you're looking for. All it takes is two or three taps to drill your way into the almanac's thousands of entries and focus on any single bit of data. Contrast that with a paper version, which requires you to skim through a table of contents or index, then flip pages and scan listings until you find the right entry. How nineteenth century!

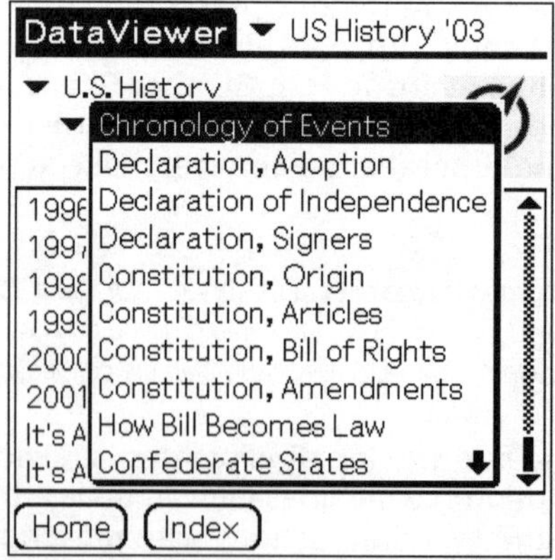

Killer Tip *After you install the program, you might expect to find an icon called Almanac, World Almanac, or something like that. Instead, the icon you're after is DataViewer, which is the name of the program used to access the almanac database files. Why? Town Compass offers a variety of other reference titles as well, including encyclopedias, dictionaries, and even a bartender's guide. DataViewer is the program required to view all Town Compass e-books.*

The 2004 World Almanac consists of 16 different sections, each a separate database file that must be installed on your PDA (along with TC-Dataviewer.prc). You don't have to install them all—you can pick and choose the ones you want. Their filenames (TC_Arts_Media '03.pdb, TC_US Facts.pdb, etc.) indicate their contents. The files range in size from about 350KB to 1.2MB, so installing them to a memory card is all but mandatory—especially if you plan to install them all.

Once you have all the necessary files installed on your PDA, tap DataViewer to start the program, and then tap the logo screen that appears. Now you'll want to choose which database to view, done by tapping the arrow at the top of the screen and selecting it from the list. Next, select a subject area from the main window, then a specific entry from the pop-up menu that appears. Tap Home at any time to return to the main screen.

FIND IT ON THE CD

The 2004 World Almanac, Handheld Edition Bundle, $11.95
Town Compass
www.pocketdirectory.com

61 Quizzler

Holy Education, Batman! It's the Quizzler!

Big test coming up? With Quizzler, you can study everything from high-school vocabulary to college SATs to firefighter training. It can even be used as a trivia game, testing your knowledge on subjects like *The Simpsons* and *The Lord of the Rings.*

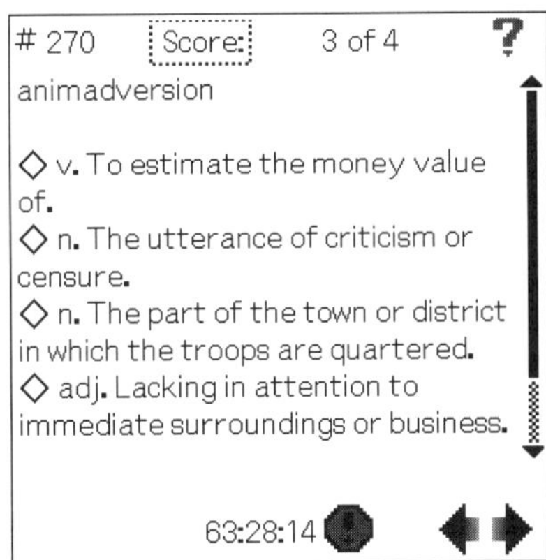

Quizzler is a freebie, believe it or not. You can also choose from a large library of free quizzes, which are available for download from the Pocket Mobility web site. These include world flags, state capitals, history, geography, and so on. To access this catalog, click the Quiz Library link, then click "Access Our FREE Quiz Library Here." (The site can be a little confusing to navigate, hence our instructions.) For quizzes like the aforementioned SAT prep and firefighter test, Pocket Mobility charges anywhere from $5 to $20.

Want to create your own quizzes? If you're up for a little rudimentary programming, you can build them right in the Palm OS Memo Pad, then import the test into Quizzler. Alternately, you can use any Windows or Macintosh word processor, copy and paste the text into a Palm Desktop (or Outlook, if that's what you use) memo, then HotSync and import the test into Quizzler. If you're planning to create your own quizzes this way, be sure to consult the Quizzler manual, which is included in the Zip file in PDF format.

Killer Tip *We've mentioned this before, but it bears repeating here. Many PDA programs come with manuals in the PDF format. To view and/or print them, you need Adobe Acrobat, a free program available from Adobe (www.adobe.com). You can also find it on the CD!*

Creating quizzes manually using the Quizzler syntax is relatively easy (again, refer to the manual), but it can also be time-consuming. If you're serious about making your own quizzes, consider buying Quizzler Maker. This $20 Windows program (a Mac version is in the works, according to the author) provides a simple interface for building quizzes and outputs them in the proper Quizzler format, ready for HotSync.

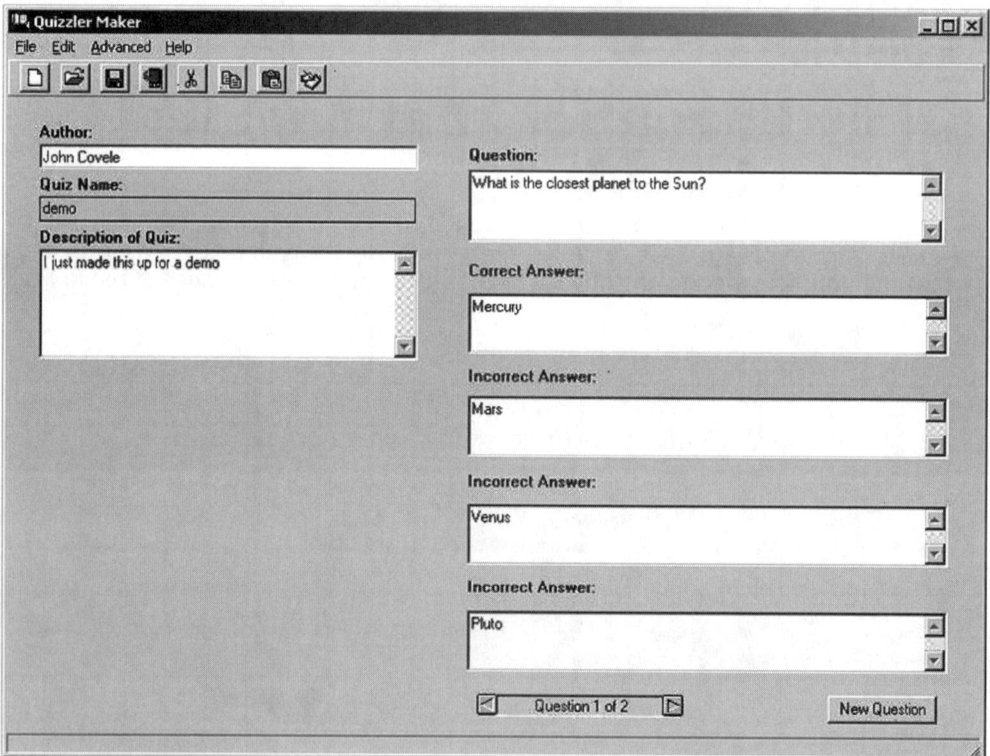

Quizzler supports multiple-choice, true/false, fill-in-the-blank, and reverse questions. It can also quiz you with flash cards. You can add pictures to quizzes (just make sure they're in JPEG format) and store quizzes on memory cards (the logical place to put your pictures as well).

FIND IT ON THE CD
Quizzler, Free
Pocket Mobility
www.pocketmobility.com

62 Alphabet Rhyme Time

Teach the Tots

Rick, who has a pair of young children, loves the idea of using his PDA to teach and entertain them. It's perfect when there's unexpected time to kill, like waiting for your food in a restaurant or stuck in line at the post office. Instead of watching the kids go berserk from boredom, you can just pull out your PDA and have some fun.

Take Alphabet Rhyme Time. It's like an illustrated (and musical) children's book, one that aims to teach kids the alphabet using an original poem. Each of its 26 pages contains a picture of an item and a line of the poem. You flip pages by tapping onscreen arrows or your PDA's scroll up/scroll down buttons.

Then there's Match Game, a freeware gem designed for kids aged 2 through 5. Match Game displays a letter, number, shape, or color in the center of the screen. Below it are three choices—your child has to tap the one that matches. Correct answers are rewarded with a big smiley face. You can find Match Game at www.pocketmobility.com.

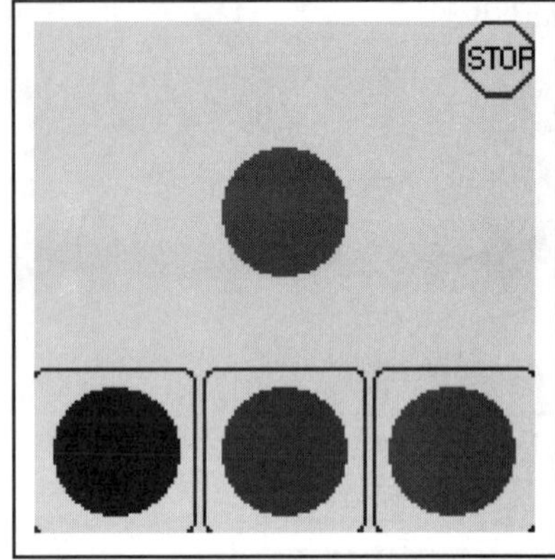

Killer Tip *Want to read your little one a story? Palm Digital Media (www.palmdigitalmedia.com), seller of PDA-formatted e-books (see Chapter 3), offers a selection of illustrated children's books—perfect for when you need to keep your kiddo occupied for a few minutes. Titles include* The Berenstein Bears, My First Real Mother Goose, *and* Puddle's ABC.

FIND IT ON THE CD
Alphabet Rhyme Time, $5
Robert Jen
www.rjen.com

63 PocketLingo Pro

A Defining Moment

Calling all students, teachers, writers, academics, and William Safire fans. PocketLingo Pro (see Figure 6-2) weighs significantly less than the print version of *The American Heritage Dictionary, Office Edition,* yet still contains all of its 130,000 words and definitions. In fact, PocketLingo Pro weighs absolutely nothing. You can cram your PDA with dictionaries, encyclopedias, and a library's worth of other heavy books, and it still won't get any heavier. How cool is that?

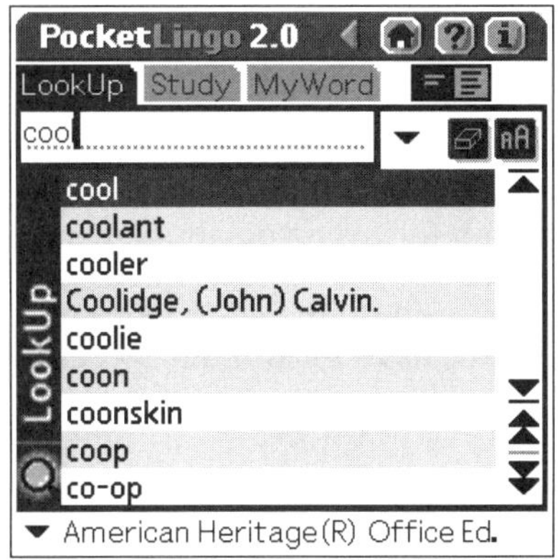

FIGURE 6-2 PocketLingo Pro contains all 130,000 definitions found in the print version of *The American Heritage Dictionary, Office Edition.*

Of course, just because PocketLingo Pro is light doesn't mean it's small. Rather, it requires a fairly large amount of memory—3.3MB, to be exact. If your PDA doesn't have sufficient internal memory to store it, or you don't want to sacrifice that much space, you'll have to install it on a memory card.

Killer Tip *PocketLingo Pro consists of three files: PocketLingo2.prc, the main application; AHD_Office2.pdb, the dictionary database; and SysZLib.prc, a system utility. The first two files can be installed directly to a memory card, but the latter must be installed to main memory for PocketLingo Pro to work. Fortunately, it's a small file—about 70KB.*

To look up a word, just start writing it. PocketLingo Pro employs a smart-lookup feature, meaning that as you enter each letter, the lookup list narrows accordingly. Thus, to look up, say, "clever," you need enter only **clev** before the word appears in the list. Once you spot the word you're after, tap it to see its definition, usage, pronunciation key, and so on.

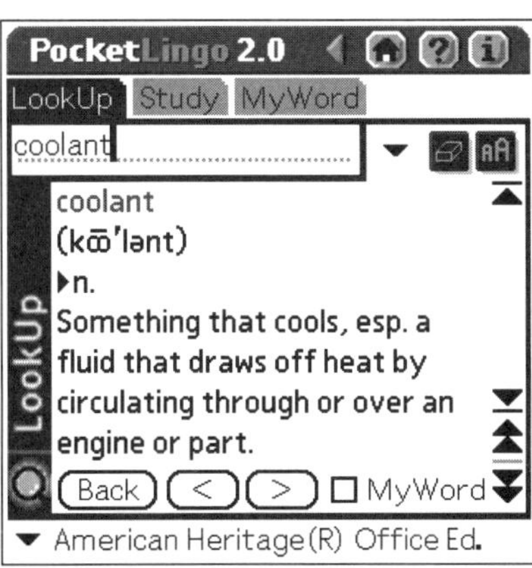

PocketLingo Pro offers two features that are ideal for students or anyone else interested in studying words. When you're viewing the definition for any entry, you can tap the MyWord check box to have it added to your personalized list of words you want to revisit and study. Tap the MyWord tab to see all the words you've added. (PocketLingo Pro comes preloaded with "Top 100 Words for High School Graduates' Vocabulary," which was assembled by the editors of *The American Heritage College Dictionary.*) Tap the Study tab for a quiz on all the words in the MyWord list.

If you're really serious about your words, check out PocketLingo College, which offers double the number of definitions. It's a whopper, though, requiring 8.6MB of storage space (peanuts if you have a big memory card).

FIND IT ON THE CD

PocketLingo Pro, $19.95
HLCSoft
www.pocketlingo.com

Improve Your PDA's Battery Life

As PDA's gain more features—fast processors, high-resolution color screens, music and video players—battery life suffers. First-generation Palm Pilots could last for weeks on a pair of AAA batteries, but modern models can peter out after just a few hours of heavy use. Fortunately, there's an easy way to extend battery life: lower screen brightness.

We know, we know, you paid big bucks for that dazzlingly bright screen, and you'll be damned if you're going to dim it. Well, which would you rather have: a dim screen or a blank one? In all seriousness, by lowering the brightness level to 50 percent—or, better yet, 25 percent—you can keep your PDA running significantly longer. Obviously, this isn't necessary if you spend most of your time near your charging cradle, but for long trips, it's a worthwhile sacrifice. In fact, we'll bet that after a few minutes, you'll hardly even notice the screen being dimmer.

Chapter 7

A Penny Saved

See if this scenario sounds familiar: Right around April 10, you figure it's time to start putting the old tax return together. To your horror, you discover that your records of the year gone by consist of a drawer full of crumpled receipts, scribbled expense reports, and unrecognized bank statements.

Doesn't sound like you? Okay, try this on for size: the check you just wrote at Sam's Club is going to bounce because you didn't know your account was overdrawn. Or this: your company won't reimburse you for the convention in Anaheim because you didn't keep adequate records of your expenses.

Whether you're "challenged" at managing your finances or simply looking for more efficient methods, Palm software developers have plenty of solutions. We've gathered some great programs designed to help you track, organize, and manage everything from checking accounts to stock portfolios.

64 Ultrasoft Money

Microsoft Money on Your Palm

Chocolate or vanilla? Coke or Pepsi? Quicken or Microsoft Money? These are the choices that have plagued humanity for as long as we can remember. We're not here to help you make decisions. But if you're among those who put their finance management in the hands of Microsoft Money, you'll want to check out Ultrasoft Money Version 3. Although it's not a Microsoft product, Ultrasoft Money is definitely Microsoft Money's mobile-finance sidekick. There's even a link to it from Microsoft's web site.

Killer Tip *If you don't use Microsoft Money (or Quicken, for that matter) on your PC but still want an effective way to manage your finances while traveling, Ultrasoft CheckBook could be the answer. The $19.95 program is pretty much a carbon copy of Ultrasoft Money, but without the desktop synchronization. (Don't worry, your data still gets backed up when you HotSync—there's just no conduit connecting it to a desktop program.)*

Ultrasoft Money emulates the most attractive features of its desktop counterpart—automatic field completion, memorized transactions, bill reminders, and so on—while taking full advantage of Palm synchronization. The software downloads all your transactions from the desktop version of Money, thus giving you a very complete picture of your finances.

At the same time, Money enables you to record transactions on-the-fly—things you buy, deposits you make, etc.—just like you do with the desktop version. The next time you HotSync, all your mobile Money entries will be updated in desktop Money (and vice versa). In short, Ultrasoft Money really is a mobile extension of Microsoft Money.

Ultrasoft Money Version 3 is designed for use with the 2002, 2003, and 2004 editions of Microsoft Money. If you're still working with Microsoft Money 98 through 2001, you'll have to work with Version 2. Fortunately, Ultrasoft's installation program is smart enough to detect which edition is loaded on your PC, so there's no guesswork required on your part. There aren't many significant differences between the two versions, other than that Version 2 limits you to 15 accounts, while Version 3 has no limit.

FIND IT ON THE CD

Ultrasoft Money, $34.95
Ultrasoft
www.ultrasoft.com

65 Pocket Quicken

Quicken in Your Pocket

Whether you live and die by Quicken or just want to get a better grip on your finances, LandWare's Pocket Quicken 2.0 (see Figure 7-1) can't be beat. This mobile edition of the desktop classic lets you record your transactions on the spot, and then updates your desktop records when you synchronize. It works the other way, too, so you're always carrying up-to-date account information. Memorized transactions and auto-completing fields are among the included Quicken amenities, and a PIN protects your data from potentially prying eyes.

Account List ▾ All Types

Name	Type	▾ Ending
401K	Invst	12,148.50
AMEX	CCard	-529.14
Apartment	Asset	200,000.00
BNZ Checking	Bank	NZ$2,574.77
Boat	Asset	17,000.00
Cash Account	Cash	185.00
Checking	Bank	1,612.04
College Loan	Liabil	-32,000.00
House	Asset	450,000.00
Balance Total		**$466,261.37**

Details | Accounts | Register | Budgets

FIGURE 7-1 Pocket Quicken looks and feels much like the desktop version, and it synchronizes with it to keep all your data up-to-date.

You need to own the desktop version of Quicken to use the Palm OS version. Fortunately, the Palm OS version supports just about every edition of the desktop version, from Quicken 99 on up through Quicken 2004 Premier. It can also sync with the Macintosh versions of Quicken 2002 and later (if you're using OS X—support for Quicken 2001 requires OS 9.22 or earlier).

This is a remarkable tool for anyone who's trying to keep close tabs on expenses or stick to a budget. The standard-issue Palm Expense program lets you record expenses, too, but it doesn't integrate with Quicken (or anything else, for that matter). Pocket Quicken updates your account balances on-the-fly, meaning that if you write a check at the grocery store, you'll immediately know if you're overdrawn. Given the fees you wind up having to pay if you bounce a check, Pocket Quicken could pay for itself very quickly.

Killer Tip *If you use Pocket Quicken to manage business expenses, it qualifies as a business expense. Therefore, you should be able to deduct the purchase come tax time. Of course, we're not H&R Block, so check with your financial advisor to make sure.*

FIND IT ON THE CD
Pocket Quicken, $39.95
LandWare
www.landware.com

66 Rebate Tracker

Keep Tabs on Those Rebates

To Rick, the only words sweeter than "after rebate" are "free after rebate." These days, rebate deals are everywhere, from your local drugstore to your local electronics superstore to Amazon.com. For the cost of an envelope and a postage stamp, you can reclaim some serious coin on a variety of purchases.

The problem lies in managing—and especially tracking—these rebates. In most cases, it takes six to eight weeks to receive your check. Unless you're one of those highly organized types, you're likely to forget which checks have arrived, when you sent in the forms, and so on. You may even forget to send the forms at all, or decide it's not worth the hassle for five or ten bucks. That's more or less what product vendors are hoping will happen—don't let them win!

Enter Rebate Tracker, a simple but effective program designed to, well, track rebates. It includes fields for all the pertinent information, such as requirements (receipts, UPC codes, and so on), product name, rebate amount, and a contact number for the rebate company. Most importantly, it records the date you sent in the rebate, so you can tell at a glance how many days it's been (and if the check is late getting to you). When the rebate arrives, you can log that date as well so you don't find yourself wondering about it a month later.

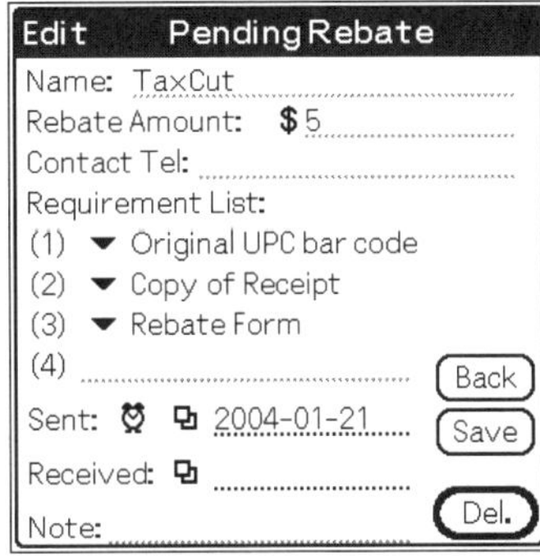

Killer Tip *Many rebate deals now include a web site where you can track the rebate's status. Use Rebate Tracker's Note field to record the site's URL so you can easily find it later. If there's no web site listed on the rebate form, use the Note field to record the promised turnaround time for the rebate (such as "6–8 weeks").*

If you really want to be organized, you can use Rebate Tracker's Report to MemoPad feature to export a summary of all your rebates to the Palm OS Memo Pad. After you HotSync, you can then print that memo from your PC and keep a hard copy of all the data.

FIND IT ON THE CD

Rebate Tracker, $8.99
XiY Technologies
www.xiy.net

67 Stock Manager

Stock Your PDA with Your Stock Portfolio

Anyone who plays the stock market knows that information is often the most valuable asset. TinyStocks' Stock Manager brings information straight to your PDA, thereby enabling you to keep tabs on your portfolio even when you're out and about.

Stock Manager ▾ All

Active New

▾ Name	▾ Price	▾ Profit
Adobe	60.8125	3932.99 ↑
AMD	30.5	75.05 ↑
Dell	45.0625	-1.16 ↓
Extreme	71.9375	27.86 ↑
IBM	115.9375	128.86 ↓
Tut Systems	41	-84.95 ↑
Wind River	37.9375	835.03 ↓

Profit:	4913.68	USD	
Profit %:	45.30%	Cost:	10845.12
Profit PA:	2.30%	Value:	15758.81

This is a robust piece of software. It enables you to manage an unlimited number of stocks across multiple portfolios. It supports different currencies and can alert you when it detects critical changes (such as price, profit, daily change, and so on) in any of your stocks. Most importantly, it updates your portfolio every time you HotSync, downloading the latest info via your computer's Internet connection. This info includes current stock price; the day's high, low, change, volume, bid, and ask; and 52-week high/low values. Stock Manager also provides valuable at-a-glance reference tools such as pie, bar, and line charts, so you can monitor your monetary distribution and stock-price histories.

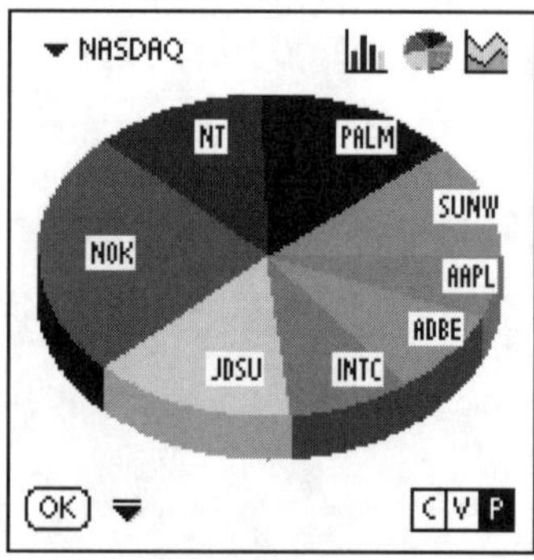

If you're lucky enough to own a wireless PDA—one that connects to the Internet via cellular service, Wi-Fi, or even Bluetooth—you can download market updates anywhere there's a live connection. That could come in mighty handy if, say, you're stuck in a meeting and tracking a volatile stock. Thankfully, TinyStocks doesn't charge extra for a subscription or anything like that—the price of the software includes unlimited lifetime updates.

To get started with Stock Manager, run the StockManagerInstall.exe program contained in the Zip file. It will install not only the desktop conduit—the bit of software that enables your PDA to communicate with your PC—but also the Stock Manager program for your PDA. (Actually, it will be installed the next time you HotSync. Just follow the onscreen instructions.) We mention this to save you some confusion—there's a StockManager.prc file in the Zip file, but you don't have to do anything with it. The aforementioned installer will handle it for you.

Killer Tip *Buy low, sell high. Just kidding—you probably already know that one. But if you're relatively new to the stock market or just need some investment strategies, pay a visit to the Motley Fool (www.fool.com). The site's mission: "To educate, enrich, and amuse individual investors around the world." How enriched you become is ultimately up to you, but the site definitely delivers on the education and amusement fronts.*

FIND IT ON THE CD
Stock Manager, $24.95
TinyStocks
www.tinystocks.com

68 Money Magazine Financial Assistant

Financial Assistance from *Money Magazine*

The only thing Rick is worse at than managing money is math. Hence his appreciation for LandWare's Money Magazine Financial Assistant, which combines a set of useful financial calculation worksheets with a variety of useful reference works, all provided by the money-savvy folks at *Money Magazine.*

The application boasts 45 problem-solving worksheets covering topics such as pricing for profit, refinancing mortgages, lease comparisons, and depreciation. Financial Assistant covers many common situations, such as trying to split a check at dinner, deciding whether to lease or buy, and figuring out how much money you can save by making extra payments on a loan. Each worksheet includes detailed instructions and usage examples.

One of Financial Assistant's most helpful features—particularly if you're still getting your feet wet in the financial and investment markets—is its 7,200-term financial dictionary. Whether you're wondering about a "parallel shift in the yield curve" or the "Joseph Effect," or you need to know the two-character ISO 3166 country code for Dominica, you'll find it here.

The Money 101 section is a great way to grow your knowledge during short moments of downtime. A series of "top 10" lists covers the key aspects of topics ranging from buying a car to investing in IPOs to saving for your kids' college. Each topic is short enough to be read in just a few minutes, yet they contain key information that can keep you from making newbie mistakes when expanding your financial activities.

Experienced investors and financial planners will find Financial Assistant useful for its numerous built-in calculators. For the beginner, casual investor, and anyone looking to get their financial act together, this program should pay for itself many times over.

Killer Tip *In the market for a more serious financial calculator? Check out Megasoft2000's MegaCalc, which is covered in Chapter 1.*

FIND IT ON THE CD

Money Magazine Financial Assistant, $19.95
LandWare
www.landware.com

Just Start Writing

Some of our favorite tips are the simplest. For instance, did you know that in most of the built-in Palm OS applications (such as Date Book, To Do List, and Memo Pad), you can create a new record without tapping the New button? Instead, just start writing. The moment you do so, you'll see a new appointment, to do item, or memo. How do you like that—we just saved you *one entire tap!*

Obviously, this tip won't work in Address Book, where the Find field is always active. When you start writing there, the Palm OS starts sifting through your contacts. And in Date Book, the just-start-writing approach creates an entry that has no time associated with it. Naturally, you can tap Details to set the information, but in many cases it makes sense to tap next to the desired time *first*, then start writing. Hey, we never said it was a perfect tip—just one of our favorites.

Chapter 8

Utilities, Tools, and Security, Oh My!

When you hear the word "utilities," you probably conjure up images of your monthly electric bill or cable statement. Or there's those four worthless Monopoly properties that Dave once conned Rick into blowing his Monopoly money on. But in the Palm universe, utilities are little programs that add capabilities to your PDA and fix niggling problems.

So follow along and we'll dig into utilities that enhance your Palm and solve annoying problems. By the time you pop out into Chapter 9, you'll have tools that eliminate those annoying duplicate records that emerge on your PDA occasionally, free up extra memory, and keep you up-to-date on the newest versions of your software. And that's not all, because we've also got some programs that let you print documents from your Palm and even beef up its security. Ready? Let's go!

69 JackFlash

Unearth Hidden Memory

One of the most common complaints that folks have with their Palm—especially when they start installing new programs and discover the treasure trove of cool apps and games at sites like PalmGear.com—is the scarcity of memory. And replacing your trusty 2MB Palm V for a more modern PDA just might not be in the cards this year. But what if you could tap into your device's Flash ROM (memory that's reserved by the OS and not usually available to folks like us) and reclaim a megabyte of otherwise unused memory for application storage? What if you could do it for just $20? Such a solution could change the way you look at an old, memory-starved PDA.

That's where JackFlash comes in. It's a small utility that moves files from system memory to the Palm's Flash ROM, a space usually reserved for core applications and system updates. Most Palm devices have anywhere from 400KB to 1.5MB of unused space in there, enabling you to extend the capabilities of your handhelds without physically adding new memory. When you run the program, you see a screen like this one:

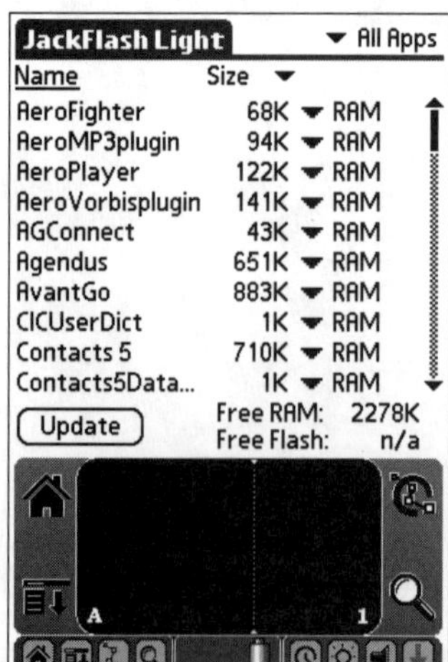

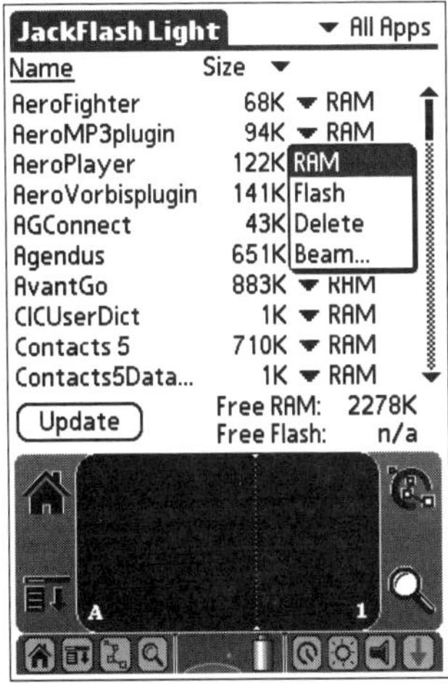

From here, you can move applications from normal RAM to Flash ROM. To do that, just tap the RAM indicator to the right of an application and choose Flash. When you tap the Update button, the programs will be copied to Flash, freeing up more ordinary RAM. Keep an eye on the Free Flash and Free RAM indicators at the bottom of the screen so you know how much memory you have available.

If you want even more memory, you might want to try JackFlash's sister program, JackSprat. For a mere $7.95, the program lets you delete some specific OS files out of Flash to free up additional memory. JackSprat removes the redundant foreign languages that are embedded in most PDAs (does anyone really need those French- and Italian-language versions of the OS that Palm stores in there?). The memory savings are significant; some PDAs can reclaim nearly 2MB of extra memory from JackSprat.

Of course, keep in mind that some devices have no Flash ROM. The best way to find out is to install the trial version of JackFlash or visit www.brayder.com for the latest news.

FIND IT ON THE CD

JackFlash, $19.95
Brayder Technologies, Inc.
www.brayder.com

70 UnDupe

Eliminate Duplicate Records

If you routinely synchronize your PDA with ACT!, Outlook, or some other third-party personal information manager, you might encounter a weird, inexplicable, and frustrating problem: duplicate entries.

In fact, if you haven't ever run into duplicate entries on your Palm, consider yourself lucky. It's a real pain in the neck to turn on your Palm and discover that, thanks to some weird HotSync oddity, your 350 Address Book entries now number 700. Sure, you could delete all the dupes yourself, but that'll take a while. And after spending hours doing it by hand, God forbid that it happens all over again three weeks later.

That's why we carry a little program called UnDupe (from Stevens Creek Software) on our Palm OS devices. No, we don't use it very often. But the one time in six months when we end up with a slew of duplicate Address Book, Calendar, or To Do entries, it pays for itself.

When you start UnDupe, it looks like this:

While the unregistered, free version will only *identify* duplicate entries on the Palm, the registered version will also *erase* them for you. Tap Find and Remove and then tap the button for the program you want to search. Tapping All eradicates dupes from all four core applications on your PDA.

FIND IT ON THE CD
UnDupe, $7.95
Stevens Creek Software
www.stevenscreek.com

71 1 Button Pro

Maximize Your Tungsten's Navigator

Your Palm's four application buttons are handy—they give you instant access to the four most commonly used programs on your PDA. But the convenience of pressing one button to launch the Address Book is addictive, and it just makes you yearn to press one button for any of your favorite programs. Of course, no one wants a PDA with two dozen buttons on the front, but there's a way to get instant access to your apps nonetheless—a utility called 1 Button Pro.

1 Button Pro lets you use the four buttons on the front of the PDA to navigate to and select pretty much any program on your Palm. Instead of each button only activating a single program, each button lets you choose from up to nine apps. In other words, you can think of the four buttons on the device as controlling four new categories for easy application launching.

It sounds complicated, but it's pretty clever and not difficult to set up. Here's what you should do:

1. On the Button Assignment screen, make sure you are about to configure the button marked 1 - Left Most. For Action, choose LAUNCH. That means this first PDA button will let you launch apps.

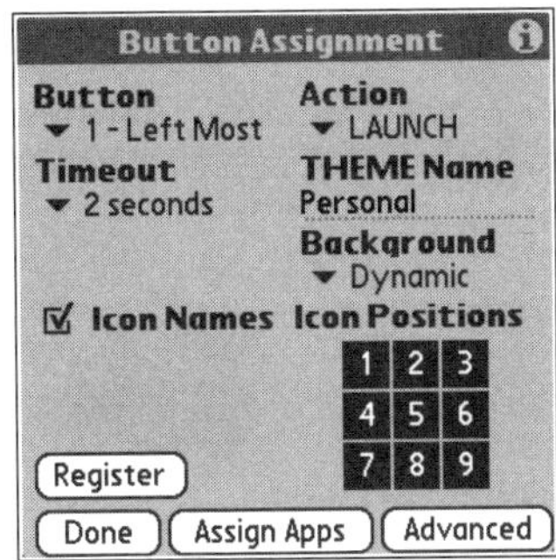

2. Leave the Timeout set to 2 seconds. That means if you use the first button to navigate to an app icon and leave it selected for two seconds, the program will launch automatically.
3. Tap the Assign Apps button at the bottom of the screen. You should see the Application Assignment page.
4. Find the apps that you want to appear in the first button category and set them to 1- Left Most using the drop-down menu. Choose any number of apps up to nine, since no more than nine apps fit onscreen at once. Tap Done when you're finished.

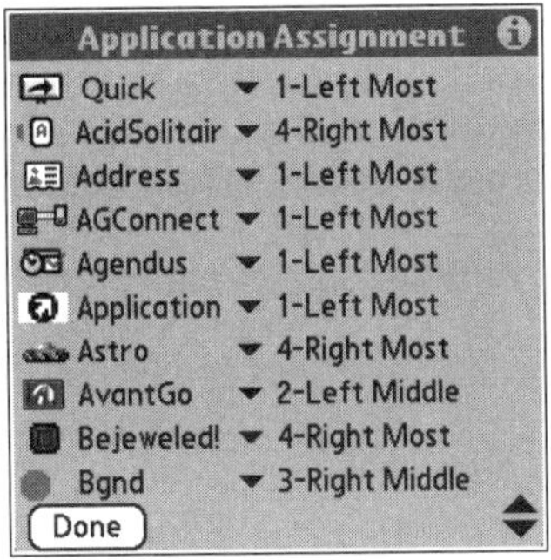

5. Tap Done on the main screen. You've now set the program for the first button.
6. Test it by pressing the first button. You should see icons for your favorite apps appear onscreen. Every time you press the first button, you select the next app.

When you find the app you want to launch, you can tap it or just wait for two seconds and the program will launch automatically.

7. You can program all four buttons in this way. Remember that you can assign all or just some of the four buttons to launch duty—it's up to you.

Killer Tip *Have a Palm with a five-way Navigator control? You can use the four-way control to select the icon you like and press the middle button to launch the app.*

FIND IT ON THE CD
1 Button Pro, $20
Evans Software
www.palmgear.com

72 VersionTracker

Keep Palm Software Current

Once you start collecting Palm applications, you might find that keeping them all up-to-date can become a part-time job. You've got games, utilities, productivity apps... and conscientious developers churn out updates, patches, new versions, and other enhancements on a pretty regular basis. Your word processor is nice, but is there a new version that doesn't crash when you switch to Bejeweled? Or is there an updated password-tracking program that lets you enter more information about each password you store? Has your favorite game been updated to support the high-res 320×480-pixel screen in your new Tungsten T3? You get the idea.

Find out with VersionTracker. VersionTracker is a web site that diligently tracks the status of thousands of applications. Visit it to see the latest version, what's new, and even download it right from the site. You can get a peek at the site's main page in Figure 8-1.

VersionTracker is a comprehensive place to find the newest details on programs already on your Palm (and on your desktop PC) or to find new applications. To find the latest on a particular program, just type the name of the app into the search box at the top of the screen. You'll get a list of all the matching applications, as in Figure 8-2.

There are also subscription versions of VersionTracker that include newsletters, automatic updates about software you own, and more.

FIND IT ON THE CD
VersionTracker, Free
VersionTracker.com
www.versiontracker.com

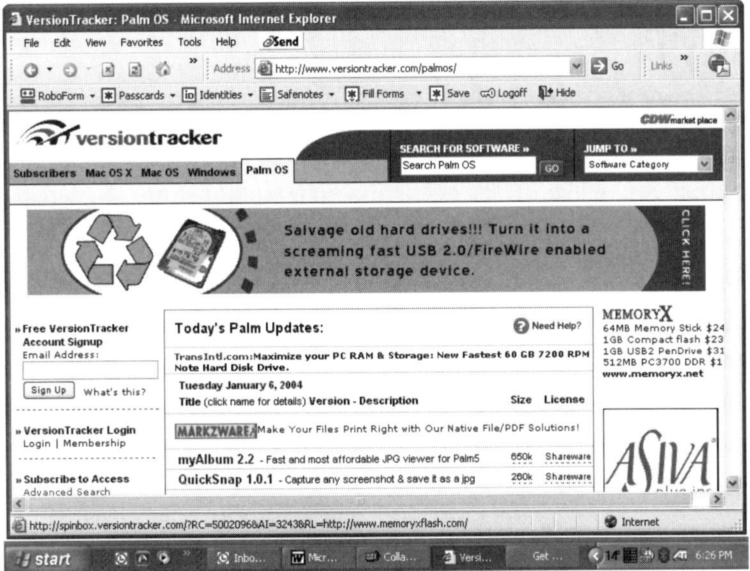

FIGURE 8-1 Version Tracker is a handy site that lets you stay on top of the latest versions of all your favorite programs.

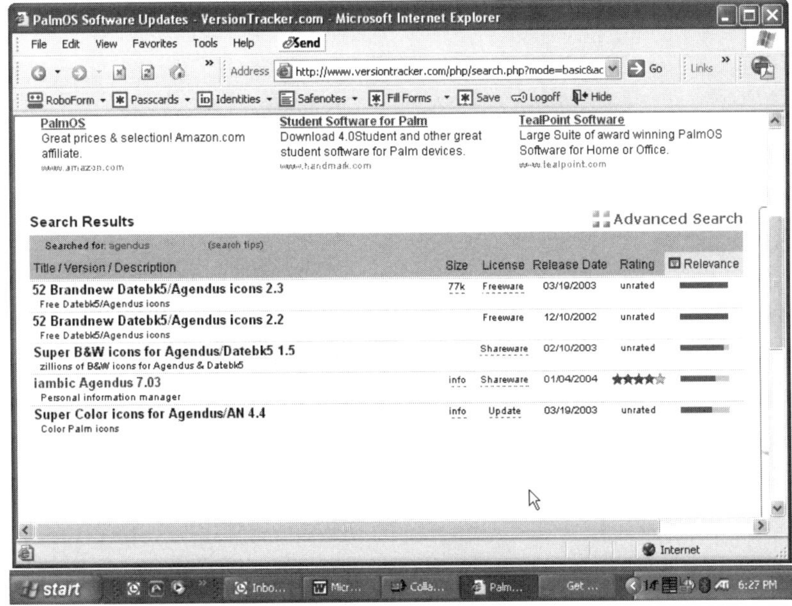

FIGURE 8-2 You can see a history of almost any commercial program—and download the latest—at Version Tracker.

73 NotSync

Simplify Software Installation

Right about now you're probably starting to really dig all these add-on programs for your Palm. If you're like us, it's becoming an addiction, and you constantly want to try the newest game, utility, or productivity application. There's only one problem: the HotSync process is too slow. It can take a minute or more to perform your HotSync (especially if you use AvantGo to grab web pages or sync large documents via a program like Documents To Go).

But who needs all that? All you want to do is install a new program. Period. So try NotSync, a clever little program that lets you quickly enable or disable a whole bunch of HotSync conduits all at once.

When you run the program, you see a dialog box like this:

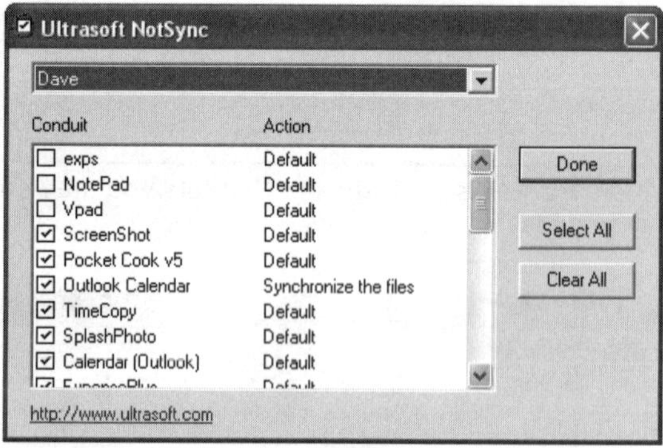

If you have more than one PDA attached to your PC, select the right one from the drop-down list at the top. Then, if you want to only run one conduit (like Install, for instance), click the Clear All button. All of the conduits are now turned off only for the next HotSync.

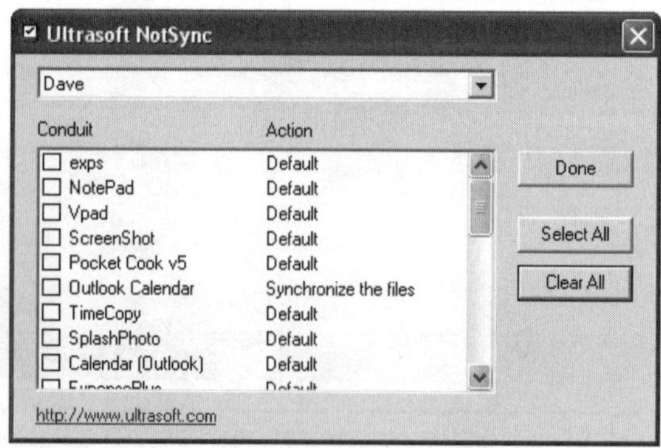

Then click the check mark for Install.

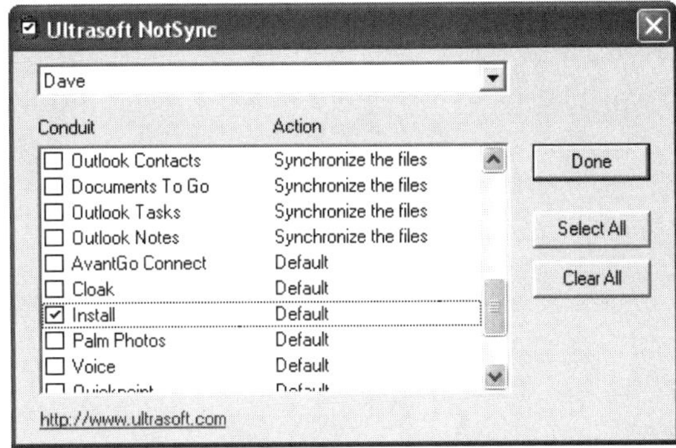

Click Done to save these settings.

Finally, you can now HotSync and only perform the Install conduit. The next time you perform a HotSync, all of your conduits will sync normally—NotSync only affects the very next sync.

If you didn't have NotSync, you'd have to open HotSync's Custom dialog box and manually deselect each one of those conduits by hand. Sure, it can be done, but it'll end up taking as long as just doing the whole HotSync to begin with. We love NotSync because it's fast and convenient. You can do it in seconds, HotSync, and then get on with your day.

FIND IT ON THE CD

NotSync, $9.95
UltraSoft
www.ultrasoft.com

74 PrintBoy

Prints Charming

The ultimate handheld PC would probably look a lot like the Palm, but with one important difference: it would have a paper-thin printer embedded inside, enabling you to print anything you see on the screen. While that's mere science fiction for the time being, this doesn't mean you can't print stuff from a Palm. Quite the contrary: armed with a print program, you can send a wide variety of documents from your Palm to a desktop printer or to a portable, pocket-sized printer.

But that's the rub—to print anything from your Palm, you need to add a print program, since one doesn't come with your PDA. We use PrintBoy, from Bachmann Software & Services, since it can print just about any kind of document to just about any kind of printer around.

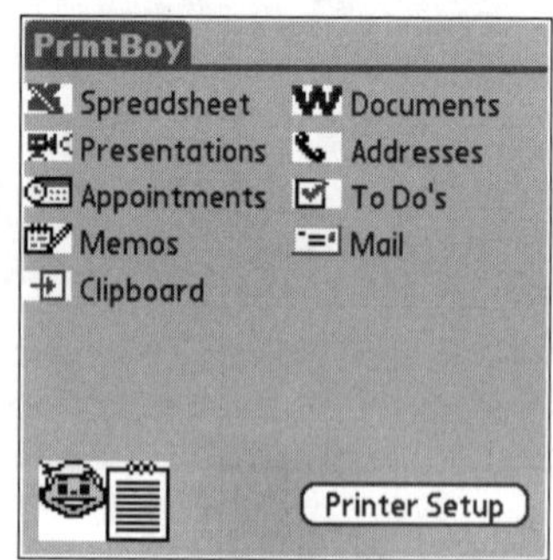

The easiest way to print from your Palm to a nearby printer is via infrared. Your Palm's IR port (the same one that you can use to beam apps and data to other PDAs) can communicate directly with compatible printers.

If you have a Bluetooth adapter for your Palm (or you have a model with Bluetooth built in), you might instead want to print wirelessly to a Bluetooth-enabled printer. As we wrote this chapter, our Bluetooth options in the printing world were quite limited, but we expect that will slowly start to change over the next few months. Even if you don't have a printer with Bluetooth built in, you can also get a Bluetooth adapter—it plugs into the printer port behind the printer and lets you access the printer from up to 30 feet away wirelessly from any Bluetooth computer or PDA.

Finally, what if you don't have access to an infrared or Bluetooth printer? That's when things can get dicey. If you own a serial port printer (such as any Apple ImageWriter), then you can plug the Palm's HotSync cradle into the printer and, with the Palm docked, send jobs to the printer.

Most Windows users don't have serial printers, though. They use parallel printers. In that case, you need a special serial-to-parallel converter (available from Stevens Creek, the manufacturer of PalmPrint).

You have another option as well. The PrintBoy InfraReady Adapter from Bachmann Software & Services is a small plug that fits into the parallel port of any printer. A small IR port turns the printer into an IR-ready device that you can use with your Palm. It's small and light, so you can carry it with you when you travel.

Intrigued? Here's a list of the most popular printers that you can use with your Palm:

Manufacturer	Printer	Style
Desktop printers with infrared		
Hewlett-Packard	LaserJet 6P	Desktop laser printer
	LaserJet 2100	Desktop laser printer

Manufacturer	Printer	Style
Portable, laptop-oriented printers		
Canon	BJC-55	Lightweight mobile printer
	BJC-85	Lightweight mobile printer
Handheld-sized portable printers		
Brother	MPrint	Handheld thermal printer
Pentax	PocketJet 200	Handheld thermal printer, compatible with IrDA adapter
SiPix Imaging	Pocket Printer A6	Handheld thermal printer

FIND IT ON THE CD
PrintBoy, $39.95
Bachmann Software & Services
www.bachmannsoftware.com

75 Cloak

Manage and Protect Important Passwords

Where do you store your most sensitive, personal data? Forget about your embarrassing Enron documentation—we're talking about usernames, passwords, credit card numbers, and access codes. Those bits of data are the keycards to your life; they deserve to be well-protected. At the same time, you need easy access. Some users compromise by storing that stuff as private records on the Palm, but a free program called No Security can expose all your private data faster than you can say "identity theft." That's right—the Palm's built-in security is, shall we say, weak.

Cloak, from Chapura, offers a better solution. A sort of digital safe for your private information, Cloak both protects your data and makes it easy to find by assembling it all in one place on your Palm. The Cloak database is protected by a robust 128-bit

Blowfish encryption algorithm. A master password is required to enter the program, and you can specify whether it's masked or visible as you enter it.

Cloak automatically closes if your Palm shuts off, making it impossible for your data to be accessed if your handheld is lost or stolen.

It's secure, yes—but is it convenient? You store your data in "accounts," each of which includes a half-dozen fields that make it easy to arrange your information:

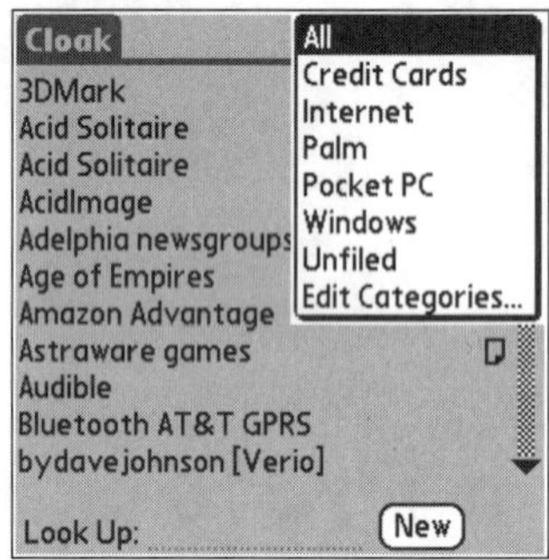

A Website account has fields for URL, username, password, and e-mail address, for instance, while the Credit Card account gives you spaces for the card number, expiration date, and PIN. If the default fields don't satisfy you, Cloak makes it easy to rename the fields (you can change the "registration number" field to "order number," for instance). Need to enter more information? Every account can have its own note as well. Cloak includes 11 account styles, so there's a ready-made set of fields for almost any data storage need, from insurance data to software registration, plus a free-form "miscellaneous" account.

The Cloak interface operates much like the Palm's Notepad. It displays all of your accounts in a list view, with just a description visible. Tap on a description and the details of the account are then unencrypted and revealed.

A desktop component duplicates the Cloak database within Windows. On the desktop, Cloak requires the same password for entry and can be used to enter or edit data—just like on the Palm. Because we often need to copy information from Cloak into other documents, like credit card numbers into web pages, for instance, we also like the way the Cloak desktop application displays the contents of the selected account without opening additional windows or dialog boxes. Indeed, we have found that Cloak is a great place to store any kind of information you need to quickly access throughout the day. Built-in security is, some of the time, just an added bonus.

The Palm makes it easy to get careless with your personal data. Cloak keeps you safe and honest—and for that reason, we think it's an essential tool for your PDA.

FIND IT ON THE CD

Cloak, $19.95
Chapura
www.chapura.com

76 PDASecure

Password Protect Your PDA

The data on your Palm is inherently insecure. If you ever lose it, all of your contact data, personal information, and more will be available to anyone that finds it. The price of the PDA is small in comparison to the loss of your data if it falls into the wrong hands.

That's why we recommend that you try a program like PDASecure from Trust Digital. It is designed to encrypt data on any PDA and requires a password for access. PDASecure offers a truly secure PDA experience by encrypting all protected data on the Palm so it can't be read on or off the device without the appropriate password. If you're fanatical about your security, PDASecure lets you choose from among a half-dozen encryption algorithms, including RC4, Twofish, Blowfish, and XOR.

One of PDASecure's most clever features, and the capability that makes it stand out from less powerful security applications, is the fact that you can set both global and application-specific passwords. As a result, PDASecure can protect all the applications via a single password at startup, or just specific applications via a local password. The main program screen shows how you can password protect specific programs and their data:

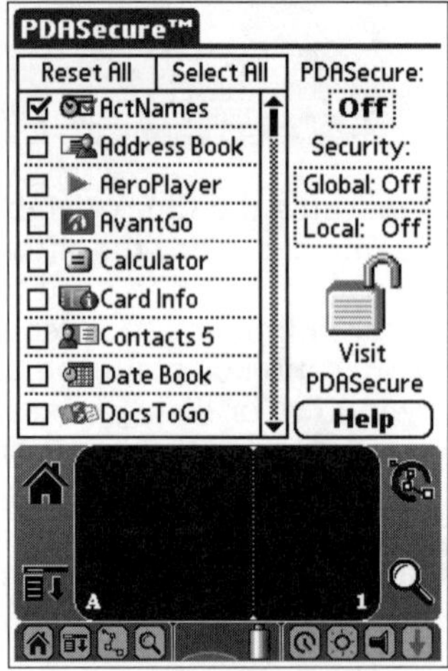

If you ever let guests use your Palm, you'll appreciate the ability to give them a "guest password" for fast and painless access to most applications via a global password, yet keep them locked out from other applications that contain sensitive or private data because they don't know the appropriate password.

You can require users to enter a password every time they use the PDA or just every few times—to get to that control, choose Options | Global Password Preferences and Options | Local Password Preferences:

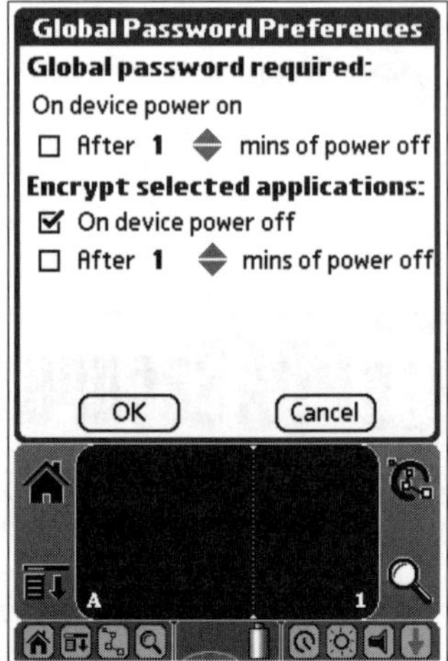

FIND IT ON THE CD

PDASecure Standard, $29.95
Trust Digital
www.trustdigital.com

Chapter 9

Just Plain Handy

This chapter is something of a catchall, a place to spotlight great products that don't necessarily fit in other categories. In these pages, you'll learn how to pack the entire World Wide Web into your PDA—and make it look good in the process. You'll learn to let your PDA wake you up in the morning by turning on the TV. You'll use it to scribble digital sticky-notes, complete with alarms that remind you when it's time to do something. And you'll never again forget an important birthday or anniversary. Ah, your PDA—it just gives and gives and gives...

77 AvantGo

The Web to Go

POWER APP

We all love the Web, and some Palm OS handhelds even let you access it wirelessly. But let's be real: the Web just doesn't fit on a three-inch screen. Enter AvantGo, a free service that not only delivers web-based content to your PDA, but also formats it to look pretty (and readable). With every HotSync, the software downloads your preselected channels—everything from news and stock reports to driving directions and movie show times—using your computer's modem to ferry the data. Pretty slick—and did we mention it's free?

To get started with AvantGo, just visit the web site and click the Get It Now button. You'll need to set up an account, download and install the software, then choose your channels. The latter step happens at the AvantGo web site: just browse the available channels and click Add when you find one you want to add. To remove channels, click the My Device tab, then click the trash can next to the channel you want to, well, trash.

If you come to really like AvantGo, you may want to increase your channel limit. By default, you get to store up to 2MB (the average channel consumes 100KB, so that would be about 20 of them). For an annual fee of $19.95, that limit increases to 8MB. That's a lot of channels, more than most users probably need.

We'd be remiss if we didn't mention two of our favorite channels. The first is Hollywood.com, which provides local movie listings. Just enter your zip code the first time you run it, and you'll always have movie times at your fingertips. The second is MapQuest (see Figure 9-1), which enables you to view driving directions created at www.mapquest.com. Just visit that site and get driving directions like you normally would, then click the Download Route to PDA button. Presto: an AvantGo channel with your directions.

FIGURE 9-1 With AvantGo installed on your PDA, you can download driving directions from MapQuest. How handy is that!

Killer Tip *Don't be surprised if it takes longer to HotSync your handheld after you install AvantGo. It takes extra time to download your channels from the Internet and transfer the data to your Palm. If you find your HotSyncs are taking too long, consider deleting some channels. You can also venture into the settings for each individual channel (located under the My Device tab on the AvantGo site) and set them to update "once daily" instead of "on every sync." That way, you'll get new content the first time you HotSync each day, but subsequent HotSyncs will skip the download process.*

FIND IT ON THE CD
AvantGo, Free
iAnywhere Solutions
www.avantgo.com

78 Room Builder

Before You Head to Home Depot

How many times has this happened to you: you get to Home Depot, all set to buy paint for your bedroom, only to realize you forgot to bring the measurements and therefore don't know how much paint to buy. Or you're at Target looking at window coverings but don't know what size curtain rod you need. Maybe you're at the furniture store and you're not sure how the new sofa will fit in your living room.

For these and other maddening situations, fire up Room Builder. This program enables you to draw basic floor plans, complete with measurements, angles, descriptions, and more. It can also calculate surface areas and square footage based on dimensions—helpful for the aforementioned paint scenario and things like ordering carpet.

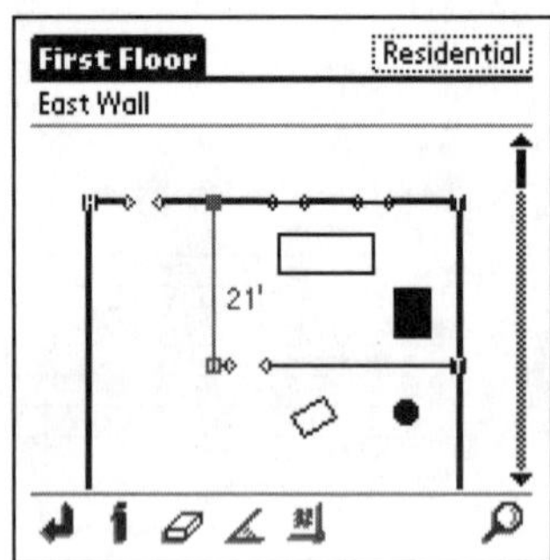

When you install Room Builder, you'll be given the option of installing an instruction manual (in HTML format, meaning you'll view it in your web browser) as well. Make sure you accept that option. Room Builder can be a bit confusing at first, but the manual explains everything in detail.

Killer Tip *If you like the idea of Room Builder but want a more robust set of tools, check out ZiPCAD|Plans (www.zipcad.com). This is a sophisticated CAD (computer-aided design) program designed to create floor plans for new and existing construction. Thus, you can also use it to design your dream house, then show the plans to your builder.*

FIND IT ON THE CD
Room Builder, $14.95
Stand Alone, Inc.
www.standalone.com

79 AirClock

The Ultimate Alarm Clock

The folks at AirSpell have come up with a clever use for your PDA's infrared (IR) port—you know, the one you use to beam your virtual business card to others. AirClock, which turns your handheld into a full-featured alarm clock, can turn on any appliance that has an IR port—TV, radio, CD player, and so on—when it's time to wake up. Just leave your PDA pointing at—and in range of—the desired appliance before you go to bed.

Now for the bad news: at press time, AirClock supported only Palm OS 4 and earlier. If you have a PDA running OS 5 or later, like a PalmOne Tungsten T or Sony Clié NX80V, AirClock's IR capabilities won't work. Fortunately, it's still a great alarm clock—and even a handy desktop clock/calendar (just leave it running in your PDA's charging cradle).

To set a standard alarm, tap Menu | Clock | Set Alarm. Now choose the time you want your PDA to "go off," and then make any desired changes to the Days setting. If you want the alarm to go off only on weekdays, for instance, tap each S (representing Sunday and Saturday, of course) to deselect them. The alarm will sound only on those days that are highlighted.

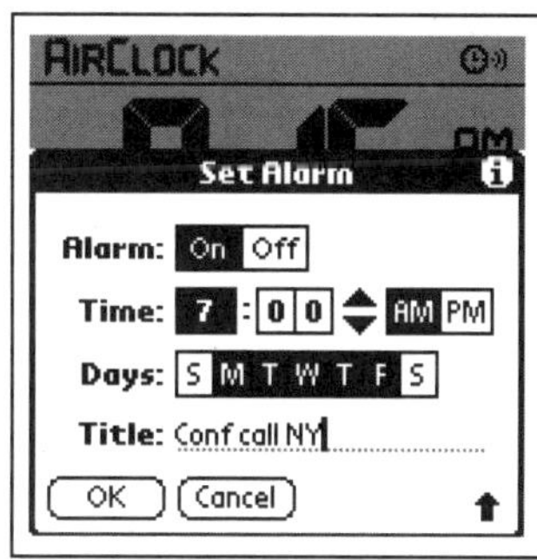

You can modify various alarm settings by tapping Menu | Options | Preferences. Tap Ringtone, for instance, to choose the sound AirClock will use for the alarm. You can also test the different volume settings and modify the duration of the alarm (how many times the sound will repeat). If you're using AirClock as a desktop clock, you can tap the Other tab and put a check in the Hourly Chime box.

AirSpell supplies an extensive manual in the AirClock Zip file, one that thoroughly explains using the software's infrared features.

Killer Tip *If your PDA uses Palm OS 5 or later, meaning you can't use AirClock's infrared features, there's a great freeware alternative. It's called BigClock, and it includes added features like a timer, stopwatch, and world clock. Find out more about it in Chapter 10.*

FIND IT ON THE CD

AirClock, $19.95
AirSpell
www.airspell.com

80 StopWatch Pro

One Sweet-Looking Stopwatch

We didn't think we could get too excited by a stopwatch program, but one look at StopWatch Pro changed all that. It's not the feature set that makes us giddy, though StopWatch Pro does have some nifty capabilities. No, what's neat about this software is that it supports skins.

Skins, in case you're not familiar with them, are fancy overlays that change the look and feel of the interface. The most famous example is the Winamp MP3 player, which you can dress in thousands of different skins—everything from Star Trek to Dave's beloved Power Puff Girls. There aren't quite that many for StopWatch Pro—in fact, there are five—but they're all very cool.

Why bother with skins? Here's what the standard StopWatch Pro interface looks like:

And here are two of the available skins:

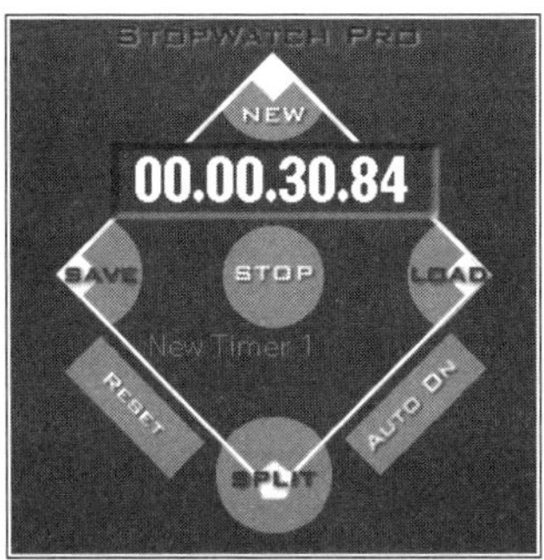

These and other oh-so-lovely skins are available for download from the Fresh Perspective Software web site. They're standard PRC files, meaning you install them on your PDA as you would any other software.

Killer Tip *Okay, so as cool as StopWatch Pro is, it's missing a few obvious features, like a countdown timer. If you need one, check out BigClock (see Chapter 10). It not only has a, um, big clock, it also includes a stopwatch, countdown timer, and alarm. Plus, it's a freebie.*

FIND IT ON THE CD
StopWatch Pro, $9.95
Fresh Perspective Software
www.fps.com

81 BugMe

Sticky-Notes Without the Sticky

BugMe has a simple premise: like electronic sticky notes, it lets you make freeform notes on your PDA and set optional alarms to be reminded about whatever you've scribbled. Think of them as Post-It notes with built-in alarm clocks.

Despite the simplicity of the concept, BugMe is packed with features. Your notes are more than just digital ink messages traced out with your stylus—you can change the color and line thickness, enter text, and even choose digital background images or document templates. Electric Pocket sells optional template packages (called Zipnotes), like a set of *Garfield* comic strip images and more business-oriented images for serious note taking. (Template packages range from $14.95 to $19.95. There's also a $29.95 package that includes BugMe and 50 Zipnotes.) There's also BugMe Viewer ($7.95), a Windows companion program that allows you to view and print your BugMe notes on your PC.

Killer Tip *Want to e-mail your notes? BugMe Messenger has all the features of BugMe, but adds the ability to e-mail your notes to others. With BugMe Messenger, you get access to the bugme.net wireless service. Equipped with a wireless-enabled Palm-powered PDA, you can send BugMe notes to other PDAs or to desktop e-mail accounts, which we did quite successfully with a Tungsten T and Bluetooth phone. It's also a handy way to use digital photos stored on your PDA—we used BugMe Messenger on a Zire 71 to enrich our notes with images from its built-in camera.*

BugMe is kind of like the Palm's Note Pad on steroids. It's a great way to take fast notes, gussy them up with colors, shapes, and text, then e-mail them to others or just alarm them for your own later use.

FIND IT ON THE CD
BugMe, $19.95
Electric Pocket
www.electricpocket.com

82 Formulas for Palm OS

Everyday Calculations Made Easy

When you hear the word "formulas," does it bring back scary memories of geometry class and Pythagoras' theorem? Fear not—Stand Alone's Formulas for Palm OS has nothing to do with geometry, and it's even more helpful than our man Pythagoras. In fact, we think a better name for Formulas would be Insanely Useful Calculators 'N' Stuff.

IUCNS (okay, *Formulas*—are you happy, legal department?) includes eight insanely useful calculators 'n' stuff:

- **Area Codes** Need to know the area code for a city or state? Want to know the major cities for any given area code? This module gives you answers to both.

- **Computer Formulas** Calling all geeks—er, we mean, computer programmers without whom we'd be miserable. With a few taps, you can convert between ASCII, binary, octal, decimal, and hexadecimal values. Hey, we've heard of one of those!
- **Currency Exchange** Formulas can convert between 19 currencies. And thanks to an included desktop conduit, you can get updated currency rates every time you HotSync.

- **Date Calculator** Need to know the number of days between two dates? Date Calculator will figure it out.
- **Latitude/Longitude Calculator** Okay, so this one isn't quite as universally useful as the others. But if you need to convert latitude and longitude formats, this is the module for you.
- **Loan Payments** Here's a quick and easy way to compute the payments and interest for any kind of loan.
- **Metric Conversion** Back in elementary school, they told us by the time we reached high school, the entire U.S. would be using the metric system. Ha! Anyway, this module converts between metric and, uh, *normal* units for things like temperature, area, and weight.

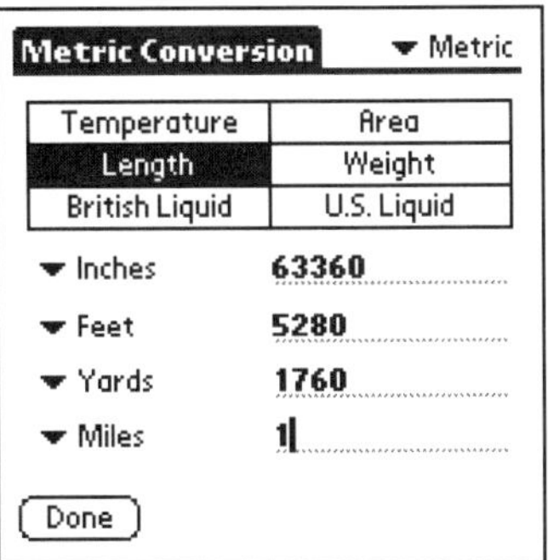

- **Tip Calculator** It's okay to admit you can't figure out 15 percent of $26.82 in your head. With this module, you can quickly calculate a tip for any amount, and for any percentage. It even gives you the total amount of your bill so you don't have to mess around with that pesky addition.

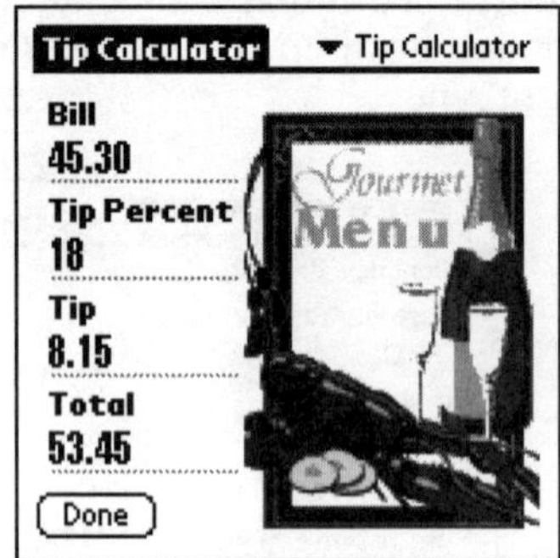

Killer Tip *Make sure your computer is connected to the Internet when you HotSync so the Currency Exchange module can successfully download the latest exchange rates.*

FIND IT ON THE CD
Formulas for Palm OS, $12
Stand Alone, Inc.
www.standalone.com

83 DateMate

A PDA User Never Forgets

Have you ever forgotten someone's birthday? How about your anniversary? These are embarrassing and even painful boo-boos. Fortunately, they need never happen again. Whether you're the forgetful sort or you just want an effective way to manage all the important occasions in your life, there's no better investment than DateMate. This program serves exactly one function: to catalog important dates and remind you of them in advance.

To get started with DateMate, tap New, and then enter the relevant person's name. If the occasion is something like a party or vacation, just use either the First Name or Last Name field to enter a description. In the Date field, you can write the date in manually or tap the little double-square icon to bring up the Palm OS date selector. For a birthday or anniversary, you can choose the year of the blessed event and DateMate will tell you how old the person (or union) is. If it's a repeating event, leave the Repeating check box checked and DateMate will remind you annually.

Alarms are one of DateMate's most valuable features. Check the Alarm box, then specify how many days (or weeks) in advance of the event you want to be reminded. If you have a gift idea in mind, tap the little dog-eared paper icon and write yourself a note.

Killer Tip *Say, can't the Palm OS Date Book accomplish more or less the same thing as DateMate? As a matter of fact, it can. For a birthday, for instance, just create a new record on the day of the event, then tap Details. Set an alarm to remind you a few weeks in advance. Then tap Repeat and choose Year. Presto: Date Book will remind you of that event from now on. It will not, however, keep track of the person's age, nor will it give you an at-a-glance view of all upcoming occasions. If you want those capabilities, you need DateMate.*

DateMate includes some useful import/export features. For instance, suppose you've been using one of Address Book's Custom fields to record birthdays for various contacts. DateMate can scan your records and import any dates it finds. It can even scan Notes. On the flip side, DateMate can export all logged occasions to the Palm OS Date Book, so you'll have them in your calendar in addition to in the program.

FIND IT ON THE CD

DateMate, $19.95
MobiMate
www.mobimate.com

84 riteMail

Scribble an E-Mail

Handwritten e-mail may sound like an anachronism in these high-text days, but riteMail enables you to send actual handwritten messages from your PDA. You can receive them there, too, provided the sender uses riteMail in any of its other iterations: Palm OS, Pocket PC, Windows, or Web.

The software is ideal for things like diagrams, maps, meeting notes, and even short messages you'd rather scribble than type. Desktop recipients need to have only an HTML-compatible e-mail program or web browser to view riteMail messages, meaning it's almost universally compatible.

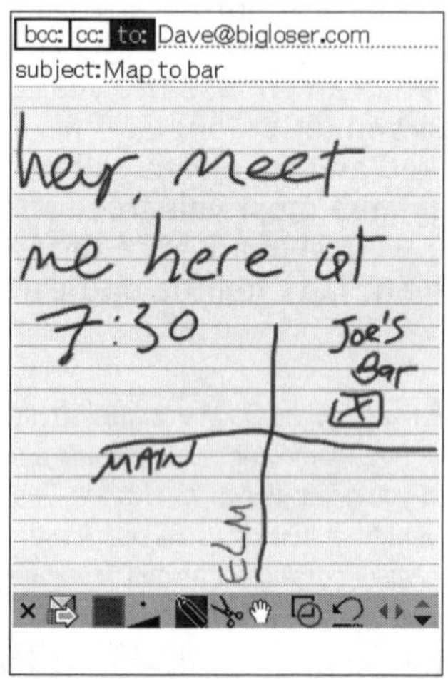

After you specify recipient(s) and subject, you simply start drawing in the scratchpad area. riteMail includes basic drawing tools, including a 32-color palette, five brush sizes, and a cool auto-shape tool for creating circles, octagons, and the like. You can even specify "paper" color and add vertical and/or horizontal grid lines. Version 2.0 supports high-resolution screens, and there's only a hint of lag between what you draw and what appears onscreen. (Hint: Write a bit slower than you normally would.) It also enables you to store received messages on a memory card.

Needless to say, sending riteMail messages is riteMail's *raison d'etre*, but it can also receive them. Unfortunately, it can't receive ordinary e-mail, so you can't rely on it as your sole client.

Killer Tip *Looking for a good e-mail program to use alongside riteMail? We highly recommend SnapperMail (www.snappermail.com), one of the most versatile Palm OS e-mail clients around. Space doesn't permit us to list all its features, but suffice it to say, it does everything.*

The only downside to riteMail is that you have to pay $14.95 per year for the service. Fortunately, the first year is included with your purchase of the software.

FIND IT ON THE CD
riteMail, $21.95
Pen&Internet
www.ritemail.net

85 HoliDates

Hoo-Ray for HoliDates

If you rely heavily on the Palm OS Date Book, you've probably noticed a fairly significant shortcoming: no holidays. The Ripple Factory's HoliDates remedies that, adding all the major U.S., Canada, and religious holidays and events to your calendar. At the same time, it gives you a list view of all the year's holidays so you can reference them at a glance, rather than having to page through your calendar to find what's coming up.

HoliDates
NEW YEARS Add year 2004-2008 holidays to Date Book or view them here.
Holiday Categories
- ☐ U.S. / Major Religious
- ☐ Canadian / Major Religious
- ☐ Christian
- ☐ Jewish
- ☐ Hindu
- ☐ Muslim

View

The program includes five years' worth of holidays, from 2004 to 2008. It takes just a few taps to add them to Date Book, where they appear as untimed events. It's equally simple to remove them. HoliDates lets you pick and choose which of six main holiday categories to install: U.S., Canada, Christian, Jewish, Hindu, and Muslim. Within each category, you can select individual holidays or just install them all in one fell swoop. HoliDates also includes major events like when daylight savings begins and tax day (April 15).

The program includes a few nice extras, like descriptions of most religious holidays and an info screen that displays the number of days left until any given holiday. And when you break down the price over five years, HoliDates costs just two dollars per year—a very fair price for filling your calendar with holiday cheer.

Killer Tip *Speaking of calendars, you might enjoy equipping your PDA with something completely different. DataViz (www.dataviz.com) Dose-A-Day calendars give you a daily helping of Close to Home (a Far Side–like comic), Dilbert, or golf. These nifty 'toons can be set to appear every time you turn on your PDA, the first time you turn it on each day, or at a specified time. There's also a "display while in cradle" option, thus giving you the electronic equivalent of a paper calendar. But Dose-A-Day doesn't start January 1—it starts whenever you install it, so you invariably get 365 days' worth of material. You can revisit missed days and even store favorites, but you can't skip ahead—a smart preventative measure against those who can't help peeking.*

FIND IT ON THE CD
HoliDates, $9.95
The Ripple Factory
www.theripplefactory.com

86 AOL for Palm OS

You've Got Mail—and AOL

If you rely on America Online for e-mail and instant messaging, you probably hate leaving home without it. AOL 3.1 for Palm puts the service in your pocket, allowing connected Palm OS handhelds to access mail and send instant messages anytime, anywhere.

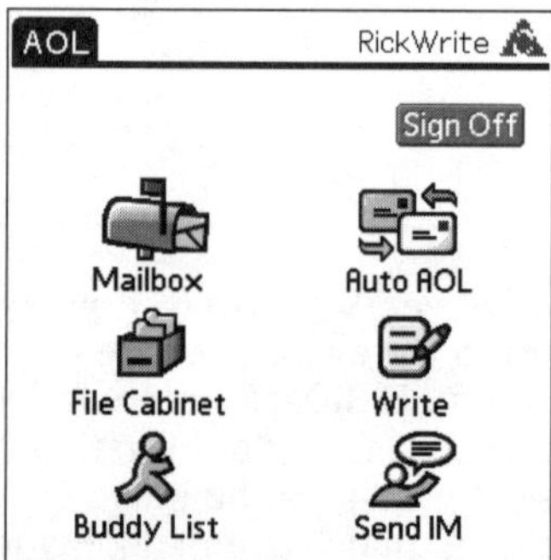

While we had some initial connection problems, eventually we got the software working on several Wi-Fi-equipped and smartphone devices. An icon-driven main menu makes it a snap to check your e-mail, compose new messages, open your File Cabinet, view and manage your Buddy List, and send instant messages to online buddies. In short, AOL for Palm works a lot like AOL for PCs. The only real rub is that this software used to be free. But if you're loathe to leave AOL behind when you leave your home or office, now you don't have to.

Killer Tip *Don't confuse AOL for Palm OS with AIM for Palm OS. The latter also costs $20 but does only instant messaging. Speaking of which, it can be slow going to type or write instant messages on your PDA. The solution? Learn Internet shorthand. Some examples: AFAIK, as far as I know; CUL8R, see you later; FWIW, for what it's worth; and our favorite: YHTBD, you had to be there. You can find a lot more timesaving abbreviations at www.10meters.com/sms_list.html.*

FIND IT ON THE CD
AOL for Palm OS, $19.95
America Online
http://anywhere.aol.com/pda

87 Freeware Pack

One Great Big Pile of Freeware

Okay, you may be wondering how Freeware Pack 1.0 made its way into this chapter instead of Chapter 10, which focuses entirely on freeware. The answer is that Rick arm-wrestled Dave and won. Freeware Pack includes some programs that are so dang handy, it would have been criminal to exclude it from this chapter.

Admittedly, you get what you pay for. Some of Freeware Pack's 20 (twenty!) programs are useful and well designed, while others are downright kooky. In the former category are programs like MileageX, which enables you to record car trips and calculates mileage based on odometer readings; Parking Lot, a simple tool for remembering where you parked; and BMI Calculator, which figures your body mass index based on your height and weight. We also like Waterlog, which reminds you to drink water (everybody needs to drink more water—we know because we read *Men's Health*), and Tip Pro, which calculates tips of any percentage and can even split checks.

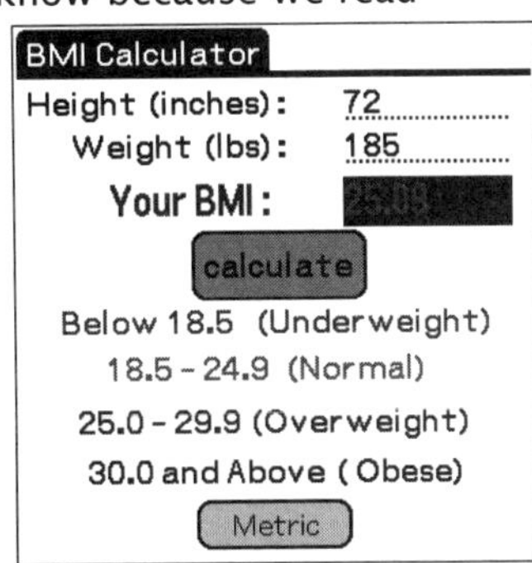

Some of the freebies are really off the wall. There's Accident Log, used to record information if you're ever in an accident (here's hoping you never need it). There's Piggy Bank, which keeps a running total of all the money you put in your, well, piggy bank. And we'd be remiss if we didn't mention My Lovers, which, um, keeps track of your love life. (Fear not, it's PG-rated, focusing on things like your significant other's favorite singers, movies, and so on.)

Killer Tip *The Freeware Pack Zip file contains additional Zip files, one for each program. Within those subsequent files, you can usually find operating instructions.*

Like we said earlier, you get what you pay for. These aren't all gems, and a few of the programs are more trouble than they're worth. But at least the price is right, and you can try them out to see if you want these kinds of capabilities on your PDA—then upgrade to more capable counterparts (just search Handango.com or PalmGear.com for related titles).

FIND IT ON THE CD
Freeware Pack, Free
PDAsoftnet
www.pdasoftnet.com/freepack

88 StreamLync 2.0

An Easier Way to Install Software

Installing new software on your Palm OS PDA isn't always the piece of cake it should be. Usually you have to download a Zip file to your PC, find the file, open it, extract the contents to a folder on your hard drive, find *that* folder, and, finally, install the proper files to your handheld. For anyone who's not particularly savvy when it comes to file management (computers don't make it easy, believe us), this can be equal parts annoying and inconvenient.

Enter StreamLync 2.0, a utility designed by the owners of PalmGear.com, our preferred site for finding and purchasing Palm OS software. Once installed on your PC and PDA, it simplifies the process of installing new programs. Here's how it works:

1. Register for a My PalmGear account (if you don't already have one), then install StreamLync from this book's CD.
2. While browsing individual software listings at PalmGear.com, look for those that have the StreamLync icon:

3. When you find something you want to download and install, click the StreamLync icon. (Don't worry, you're not buying anything.)

4. If the program supports StreamLync 2.0, you'll immediately be taken to your PalmGear page. HotSync, and you're done! If the program doesn't support 2.0, you'll see a dialog box asking if you want to Open or Save the file. Choose Open.
5. StreamLync will then ask you to choose a user. Select the HotSync name for your handheld. (This step can be eliminated—read on to learn how.)

That's all there is to it! After the file has downloaded, just HotSync your PDA.

You may want to make some adjustments to StreamLync's settings (which affect only those programs that aren't compatible with StreamLync 2.0). On your PC, click Start | All Programs | PalmGear.com | StreamLync Settings. This opens a small dialog box. Notice the three check boxes near the top:

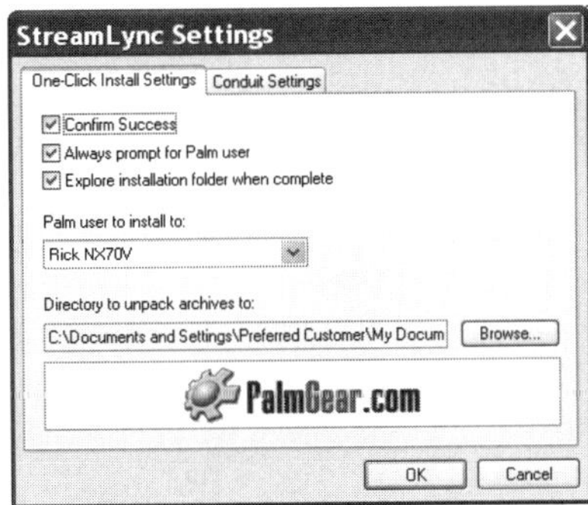

- **Confirm Success** Don't want StreamLync to notify you every time a program has downloaded successfully? Uncheck this box.
- **Always prompt for Palm user** If only one PDA is connected to your PC, there's no reason for StreamLync to ask you to choose a user every time. Uncheck this box and you can skip a whole step!
- **Explore installation folder when complete** When checked, StreamLync will open an Explorer window to let you see what files were contained in the download—helpful for finding instructions and perhaps some additional files (like special music for a game) that weren't installed by default.

FIND IT ON THE CD

StreamLync 2.0, Free
PalmGear.com
www.palmgear.com

Saving Scratched Screens

Scratches happen. They happen most often when your stylus hits a piece of dust or grit. That's why it's important to keep your screen as clean as possible (we recommend a daily wipe with a lint-free, antistatic cloth). Better still, take a few preventative steps:

- **Tape** A piece of Scotch Magic Tape 811 placed over the Graffiti input area (where most scratches occur) not only makes existing scratches less tangible while you're writing, but also prevents future scratches and provides a tackier writing surface. (Obviously, you don't want to use this tip if you use a Garmin iQue 3600, PalmOne Tungsten T3, Sony Clié NX80, or another model that has a virtual Graffiti area.)
- **Screen protectors** We're partial to plastic overlays that protect the entire screen. One solution is a product like the BoxWave ClearTouch (www.boxwave.com). It won't remove scratches, but it will prevent them and, like the tape, make them less pronounced. Also, be sure to check out www.freescreenprotectors.com, where you can find overlays for a wide variety of PDA models. Enter **FREESP** when you check out, and you'll pay only for shipping.
- **PDA ScreenClean** Fellowes' (www.fellowes.com) wash-and-dry system may remind you of those wet-nap packets you get in those greasy-spoon restaurants Dave likes. One packet contains a wet cloth you use to wash and wipe the screen, the other a dry cloth you use for drying and buffing. These won't repair scratches, but they will remove all the dust and grit that can lead to them, and leave your screen looking pristine.

Chapter 10

Fabulous Freebies

Is any word in the entire English language so sweet as "free?" Listen to the sound of it: free! It rolls off the tongue in a way that suggests you're getting something for nothing. And in the world of software, free stuff totally rocks. Just download, install, and rock and roll—no trial versions, no expiration dates, no credit cards changing hands. That's why we decided to wrap this book up with a look at a dozen or so totally free applications you can try out on your Palm OS device and keep, if you like them, forever.

The stuff in this Fabulous Freebies chapter runs the gamut of cool things you might want for a PDA—a better alarm clock, some games, a reference dictionary, an image viewer, and lots more. All of these programs were written by enthusiastic, dedicated programmers who wanted to release something for fellow Palm OS fans, but who wanted nothing in return. That's cool, don't you think? So if there's something you like in this chapter, why not send the author a quick e-mail thanking him or her for the program?

89 BigClock

It's an Alarm, It's a Stopwatch, It's a World Clock

A clock? For your PDA? Since it already has one built in, you must surely be wondering why we're suggesting that you add another. Well, here's the deal: You can set alarms with the Palm, but the somewhat anemic built-in alarm system isn't terribly useful in many situations. Instead, you should install BigClock (see Figure 10-1). This application displays the time, has a stopwatch-style timer, and has four independent alarms. It also lets you easily change time zones.

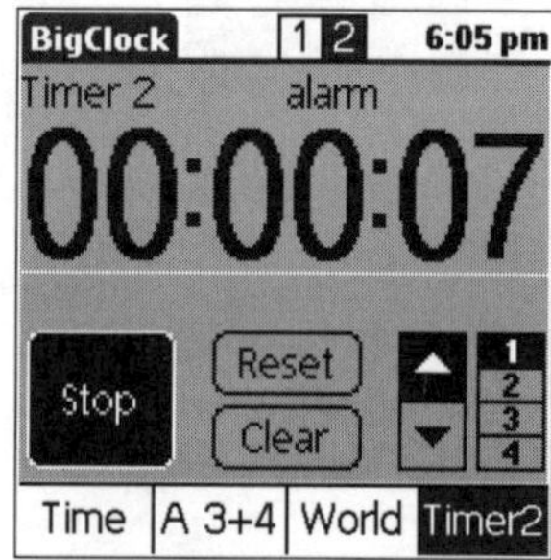

FIGURE 10-1 BigClock has multiple alarms and time zones—the perfect companion for life on the road.

BigClock's alarm is good enough to serve as your morning alarm clock, either on its own or as a safety backup to a hotel wake-up call. (Dave always uses BigClock because he doesn't trust hotel wake-up calls. He's somewhat neurotic in this way.) To use BigClock's alarm function, follow these steps:

1. Start BigClock and tap on the Alarm tab at the bottom of the screen. You have four different alarms available. We'll set Alarm 1.
2. Tap the Alarm 1 title at the top of the screen and rename it **Wake Up**.

3. Set the time you want to wake. Tap on the top half of a number to increase its value, tap the bottom half to decrease it. Do this for both minutes and hours.
4. Make sure the am/pm indicator is set to am for your morning alarm. Tap it to switch between the two.
5. Tap the day or days that you want to alarm. If the day is highlighted in black, it's selected.
6. To enable the alarm, tap the large check box to the left. The alarm will now trigger at the designated time.

You should test your alarm before trusting it to get you out of bed the next morning.

You can set BigClock's alarm to snooze—that is, re-alarm after a few minutes if you want to nab a few extra minutes of sleep. To enable the snooze feature, choose Settings | Alarms from the menu. In the Alarm dialog box, tap the number of the alarm you want to set and then tap the Snooze check box. You can set how long the snooze will last (a common length is about ten minutes, if you're setting a wake-up alarm) and how many times the snooze will go off before turning off completely. When the alarm goes off, tap anywhere on the Palm screen (except the button to turn off the snooze) and the snooze resets the alarm to go off again a few minutes later.

Killer Tip *The snooze only works if you tap the screen. Since the alarm will only sound several times and then shut off, BigClock runs the danger of letting you fall asleep without actually tapping the screen to activate the next snooze cycle. To avoid oversleeping, you should modify the alarm sound so that it chimes for a long time. To do that, choose Settings | Sounds and then set the repeat value to a very large number—like 100. That should be enough time for you to rouse from sleep and tap the Palm.*

FIND IT ON THE CD
BigClock, Free
Jens Rupp
www.palmgear.com

90 Vexed

Vex Your Brain with Cool Puzzles

POWER APP

Vexed. This infuriatingly addictive game is about as good as puzzle games get. The premise is simple: move blocks around on the screen in an effort to get identical ones to touch and annihilate each other, thus clearing the board. The execution is fiendishly complex, though, and that's what makes this game so cool—and so surprising that it's free!

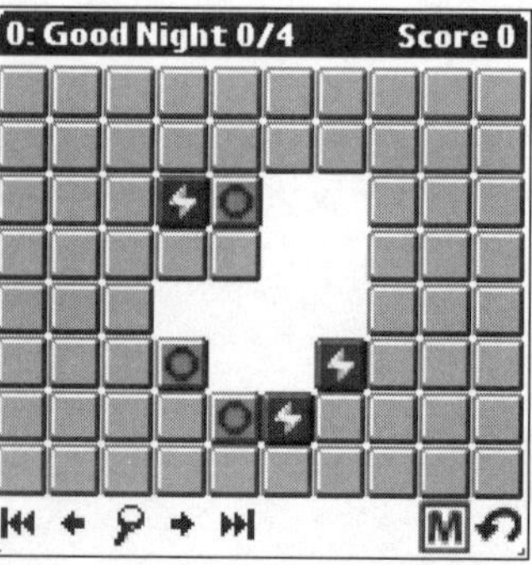

How does it work? Let's walk through the first level to give you a taste of the game. When you start, it has two sets of three blocks, arranged like this:

Tap and drag the top *O* block to the right, so it falls:

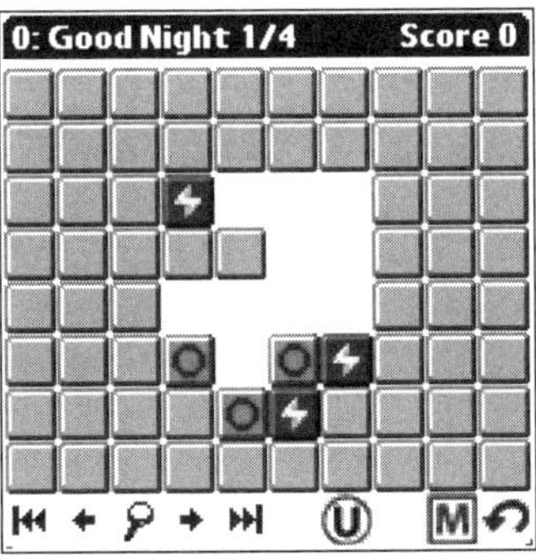

Now drag it to the left. When it touches its two clones, all three will disappear:

Finally, drag the top *Z* block to the right until it falls and obliterates the two similar blocks below. You've cleared the board and the game moves on to the next level.

That first level was very easy, but keep in mind that the order in which you move blocks means everything when you need to delete every single one from the screen—so you can't simply eliminate a pair of similar blocks if it's convenient if a third block is positioned elsewhere on the screen.

There are lots of additional levels and expansion packs available, so Vexed is sure to keep you busy for a long time.

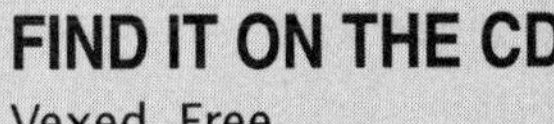

FIND IT ON THE CD

Vexed, Free
James McCombe and the Vexed Team
vexed.sourceforge.net

91 Patience Revisited

The Ultimate Solitaire Collection

Every version of Windows since about 1990 has come with a version of Solitaire built in. While the rationale might have originally been to provide some mouse training for new Windows users, let's face it: Solitaire is the perennial time killer when you're working up the ambition to start your next project. It's a great way to ease back into work after lunch. And who among us can claim to have never played a little Solitaire during a teleconference?

It's a shame, then, that such a great little game as Solitaire didn't come bundled with the Palm OS. You can buy a commercial version of Solitaire, of course, but why bother? Patience Revisited gives you 21 different versions of the solo card game for free. You can see some of those games here:

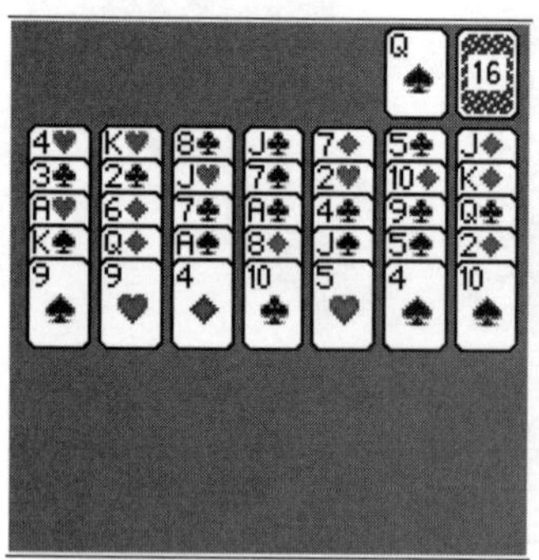

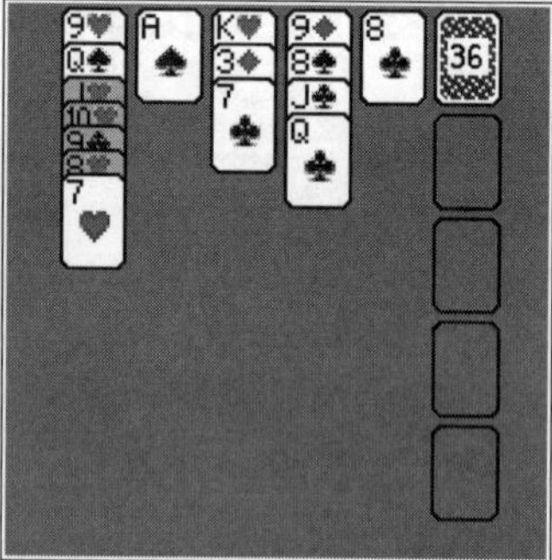

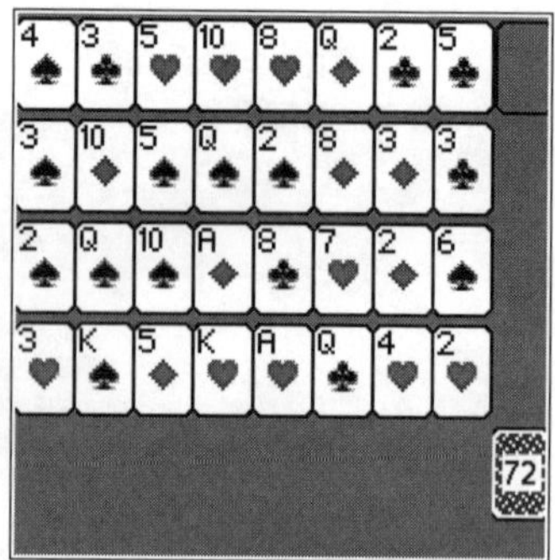

The New Game screen is awash in versions of Solitaire:

New Game

Short Games

Aces High	Golf	Vegas
Canfield	Klondike	Wish

Long Games

Calculation	Montana	Tabby Cat
Eight Off	Spider	Towers
Freecell	Spiderette	Yukon
Stalactites	Ms Milligan	40 Thieves
Pict. Gallery	Tarantula	Roy'l Cotillion

Ok Rules Cancel

Notice that you can tap the Rules button at the bottom of the screen to see a solid synopsis of how each game is played:

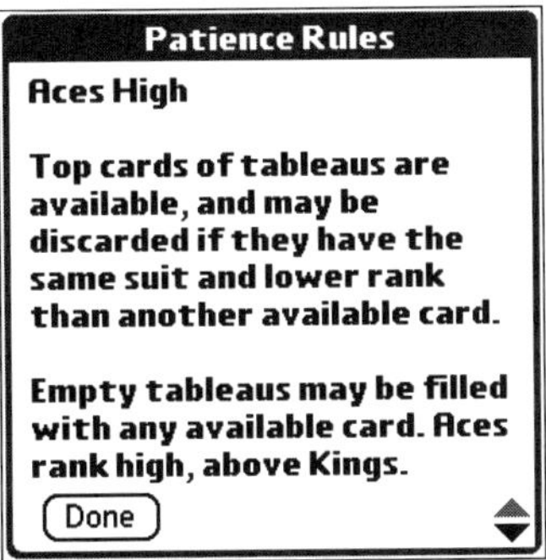

Once in a game, card movement is exactly how you'd expect: drag and drop them to stack your cards and build your tableaus. Be sure to check the game menus; there are options for autoplay (in which logical moves are made for you) and a slew of game preferences.

FIND IT ON THE CD

Patience Revisited, Free
Paul Close
www.palmgear.com

92 Pocket Blackjack and Pocket Video Poker

Cheaper than a Trip to Vegas

Dave and Rick travel to Vegas about once or twice a year for those technology trade shows you read about in the paper. COMDEX and the Consumer Electronics Show are great opportunities to see robot dogs, Internet-enabled microwave ovens, and remote-controlled shopping carts. But it's also an opportunity to saddle up at the blackjack table and lose a month's pay by being really bad at cards.

If you don't want to risk real money on games of chance, you can get the Vegas experience for free right on your Palm. We've found a pair of programs that will make you feel like you're sitting in the Bellagio.

Pocket Blackjack is easy to play. Start by placing a bet—tap the chips in your pot until you have the amount of money you wish to wager.

When your bet is ready, tap the Deal button. From there, just Hit or Stand, and, when appropriate, Double or Split your hand.

When you tire of Pocket Blackjack, try your hand at Pocket Video Poker. Here's what you need to know: Jokers are wild and you have a maximum bet of five dollars. Place your bet (every time you tap the Bet button, you add a dollar to the wager) and then tap Draw.

Tap any cards you want to keep—you'll see the word "Hold" appear under the card. Then tap Draw again to finish the hand.

Note *If you're not keen on visiting an online casino, you should probably avoid the registration link for this game—it takes you right into a web-based casino.*

FIND IT ON THE CD

Pocket Blackjack and Pocket Video Poker, Free
GoldPalmCasino, Inc.
www.palmgear.com

A Web Sync Can Save the Day

Recently, Dave was traveling with his Palm and it suffered a catastrophic failure. All the data was lost, and he didn't have a backup with him. What did Dave do? Did he resort to managing his schedule on pen and paper? No, of course not! He resynced via the Web.

You may not realize this, but Yahoo's Calendar and Address services can be synchronized to your Palm OS PDA via a little program called Intellisync for Yahoo. Here's the deal: Sync your Palm and PC normally. But then also sync the Palm with Yahoo. When you travel, if anything untoward happens to your PDA—the battery dies, a hard resert costs you your data—all you need is a portable HotSync cradle and any PC with Internet access. Just sync the PDA with your Yahoo account and you'll be back up and running in no time. Where do you find all this? Just log in to Yahoo and go to the Calendar page. Look toward the bottom of the screen and you should see a Sync link. Follow the directions to install Intellisync and you're in business! (And yes, it's free. Free, we say!)

93 HandyShopper

Grocery Lists to Go

If you're like us, you probably keep a notepad on the front of your refrigerator for tracking shopping lists. You've got a Palm, though, so why not use it instead? HandyShopper can keep a list of all the items you typically shop for. When you shop, you can use it as a checklist to cross off items you've bought. So it's a great, all-in-one shopping list app—and it does a number of other things as well.

Ready to go shopping? Here's how to use HandyShopper:

1. Add new items to your database by tapping the New button and filling out the form for the items you want to buy.

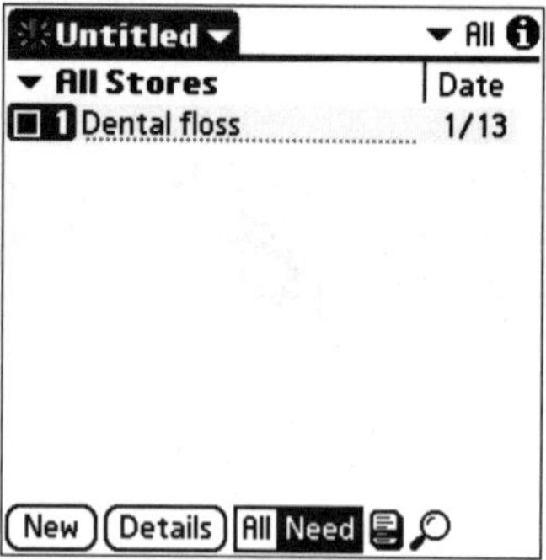

2. If you already have previous items stored in the database, you can add them to your current shopping list. Tap All to see all the items, and then tap the dot to the left of an item to add it to your list. When you're done adding old items to your current shopping list, tap Need to see just the items you want to buy now.

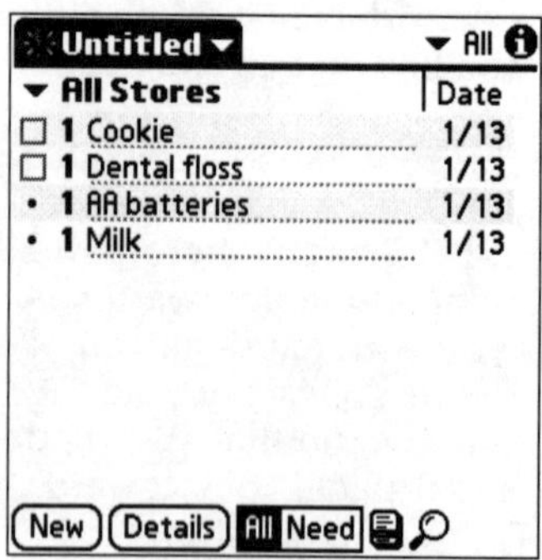

3. When you get to the store, check off items as you buy them. They'll get crossed off the list.

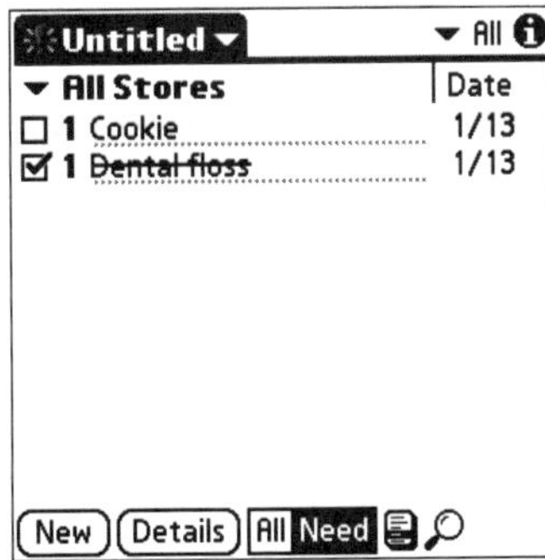

4. When you leave the store, you can tap the button to the right of the Need button and select Checkout from the menu. Bought items will disappear from the shopping list until you need to buy them again.

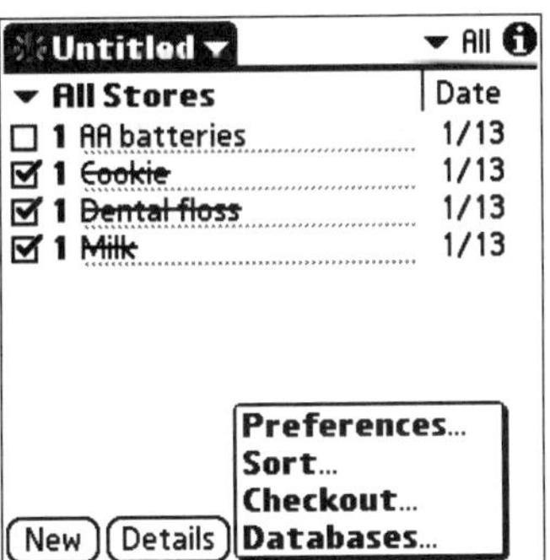

Killer Tip *If you want to make it easier to find these items in the store, tap an item and then tap the Details button. You can enter price, quantity, and even location within the store.*

All that's great, but for us, one of the most interesting features is its ability to compare the actual price of two similar products. Suppose you're buying tissue paper that costs $4.99 for 10 ounces, and the other brand sells 12 ounces for $5.49. Which is the better deal? Find out by choosing Record | Best Buy from the menu and entering the price and quantity in the Best Buy dialog box. For the record, you should buy the second item, since it's cheaper by about four cents per ounce.

FIND IT ON THE CD
HandyShopper, Free
Christopher Antos
www.palmgear.com

94 DiddleBug

Like BugMe, Only You Don't Have to Pay for It

Few inventions in the twentieth century have had as much impact on office life as the ubiquitous sticky note. The desktop computer and electricity don't hold a candle to those yellow squares of paper that, in some cubicles, actually replace wallpaper.

BugMe is an electronic alternative to sticky notes on your Palm. Not only do BugMe notes accommodate text and graphics, but they do things that real yellow stickies only dream about—like automatically reminding you about their contents. The only problem is that BugMe costs money. DiddleBug, on the other hand, does not.

DiddleBug, at its heart, is a sketching program. You can draw free-form shapes on the Palm screen by drawing directly on the screen with your stylus. You can also jot down short notes in "digital ink." But while the commercial BugMe supports color, DiddleBug is black and white only. That's unfortunate, perhaps, but did we mention it's free?

All that is cool, but not extraordinary. DiddleBug is unique in that it allows you to attach alarms to each of your notes. At a preset time, your DiddleBug memo pops onto the screen, complete with a snooze button, and vies for your attention.

Here's how the program works:

1. If you don't immediately see a blank screen, create a new note by tapping the New button at the bottom left of the screen.
2. Draw anything you like on the screen using the various pen tools at the top of the screen. You can adjust the pen thickness and style, as well as switch to an eraser to selectively undo your strokes.
3. There are two ways to add text to your note. You can draw using digital ink or tap the Note button at the top left of the screen and enter any text you like using Graffiti.

4. When you're done, you can set an alarm to be reminded about the note. Tap the Alarm box at the bottom of the screen and choose any sort of alarm you like. You can set it to go off in a certain number of minutes or choose Absolute, which opens a Set Alarm Details dialog box. Use it to set an alarm for any date and time you choose.

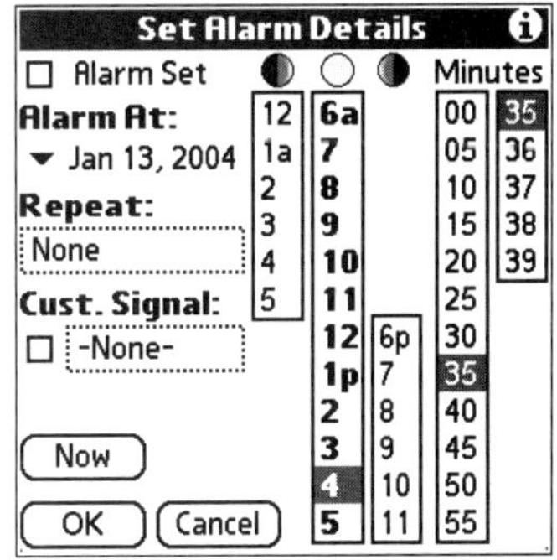

FIND IT ON THE CD

DiddleBug, Free
Peter Putzer
www.palmgear.com

95 HappyDays

A PDA User Never Forgets

One of the benefits of having a PDA is simple—it helps you remember things. So why is it that despite your PDA, you still forget all those birthdays? The Palm's Address Book isn't really set up to track birthdays—that's why.

No problem. That shortcoming is easily solved with a little program called HappyDays. After you install it, you'll be able to quickly and easily track all the key dates that have for too long gotten you in trouble with your spouse, family, and friends.

When you first install HappyDays, it probably doesn't tell you anything at all. If you want to see more than a blank screen, you need to make a few key changes. Try this:

1. Switch to the Palm's Address Book.
2. Choose Option s| Rename Custom Fields. These are the four fields at the end of each Address Book entry that you probably ignore. In the Rename Custom Fields dialog box, change the first field to **Birthday**. Click OK to close the dialog box.

3. Choose an entry in the Address Book and edit it. Scroll to the bottom, and you'll see that one of the four custom fields now reads Birthday.
4. On the Birthday line, enter a date, like **5/15/1966**. Tap Done to save the data.

5. Switch to HappyDays, and you'll see that the program has found and is displaying the date in the program.

6. Tap the entry and you'll get additional information, such as the person's exact age and the day of the week that the birthday next falls on. Cool, no?

FIND IT ON THE CD

HappyDays, Free
Jaemok Jeong
www.palmgear.com

Manage, Beam, and Delete Your Files

Not everyone likes to tinker with the files on their computer, but for those who do, operating systems such as Windows and the Macintosh give tons of options for digging into the nuts and bolts of the PC to see, inspect, delete, and move files. The Palm OS is not nearly so easy to use for tinkering.

As a result, a lot of developers have made file browsers for the Palm that let you dig right into the guts of your PDA and manage files. FileZ is one of them and, as you can guess from its location in this chapter, it's free.

When you start FileZ, you see a few main options and a snapshot of your free memory and battery health. Tap on the memory or battery bar to cycle through different views of the same data.

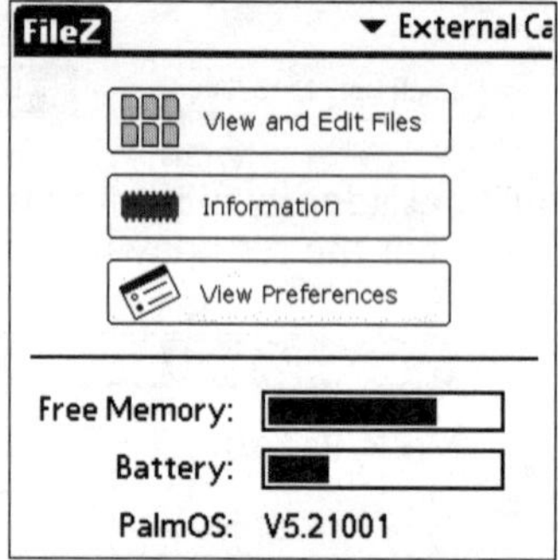

Want to see more? Tap the View and Edit Files button to see a list of every file on your device—hidden, system, or otherwise. This is the PDA that Palm doesn't want you to see! You can select files by tapping and then use the File menu to beam, delete, or move the files.

You can also switch between the files stored on your Palm itself and the files on a memory card—just select between PalmCard and External Card in the category list at the top right of the screen.

FIND IT ON THE CD

FileZ, Free
Nosleep Software
www.palmgear.com

Drawing and Doodling

You're probably wondering why you might want to paint on a handheld computer so small that it fits in your pocket. Well, in the world of computers, the answer is often "because you can." Programmers have never let something as silly as a technical limitation get in the way of doing something, so when PDAs first came out, programmers seemed to scramble to become the first to create a paint program for their favorite handheld PC.

But, aside from that admittedly flippant answer, the capability to sketch things out on your Palm is a handy feature. You can draw a map to sketch the way to lunch, outline a process, or design a flowchart. You can jot a quick note to yourself in digital ink. You can tap into your creative side when you're between meetings. You can also just doodle—use the PDA as a high-tech Etch a Sketch for those boring times when you're waiting for the train or pretending to take notes in a meeting.

Painting on your Palm is fun and productive, but you need to remember these limitations:

- Palm models vary in resolution from 160×160 pixels all the way up to 480×320 pixels. The more pixels you have, the better, but even the highest-resolution devices don't give you a lot of room in which to draw. After your images are transferred to a PC, you'll find that they're still quite small. So, drawing something on the PDA you later plan to export to, say, a PowerPoint presentation generally isn't a practical plan.
- Forget about printing your works of art. That means, in general, what you draw on the screen pretty much stays on the screen. If you *can* print your work of art, it'll print just as rough and jagged on paper as it looked onscreen.

Many painting and drawing applications are available for the Palm. Indeed, if you're an adventurous sort of person, search the archives at PalmGear for painting programs, and you'll be amazed by what you find. Nonetheless, our favorite is a free program called Sketcher. You can see it here:

So what can you do with it? Quite a bit. Sketcher has a slew of drawing tools on the right side of the screen and supports a full color palette. There's an eraser and different backgrounds, like ruled paper, a dotted grid, a picture frame, and a black "chalkboard." You can even set alarms (like DoodleBug) and beam your completed images to other Palms.

If you like Sketcher, you might want to also try Sketcher Export. It's a Windows application that lets you convert images from your Palm to BMP files that you can include in other Windows applications or even print.

FIND IT ON THE CD
Sketcher, Free
Palmetto Logic
www.palmgear.com

98 Loan Helper

A Little Help from Loan Helper

You know the feeling: You're sitting at the car dealership while the salespeople wander in and out, "checking with their managers" and "seeing what they can do for you." It's all very unnerving, frustrating, and scary. After all, do you even know what the monthly payments will be before you enter the finance office? You should. Knowledge is power, and you need all the power you can get when buying a new car.

That's why we recommend Loan Helper, a free loan calculator that lets you determine every aspect of the loan before you even step foot in the car dealership.

When you fire it up, just enter what you know—like the car's base price, the trade-in value of your old car, the amount of your down payment, and so on—and leave the thing you're looking for (like the monthly payments) blank. Tap Compute and get the answer—that's all there is to it.

Notice that there's a list to the right of the Compute button. There you can fine-tune the calculator by choosing what to solve for. If you're interested in knowing how much car you can afford based on your down payment and your preferred monthly payments, select base price from the menu and enter values accordingly.

Killer Tip *Want to compare car deals? You can create up to 12 concurrent loans and switch among them using the arrow buttons at the bottom of the screen. To create a new loan, choose Record | New from the menu.*

FIND IT ON THE CD

Loan Helper, Free
CobraPit
www.cobrapit.net/LoanHelper

99 Noah Lite

Look In the Dictionary Under "Free"

Have you ever packed a bunch of books into a backpack and carted them around all day? It's hard, we know. But if you pack a slew of books onto a PDA, it doesn't get any bigger, fatter, or heavier. And therein lies the key advantage of carting around reference books on a Palm.

If that sounds appealing, then you'll want to install Noah. It's a free dictionary for your PDA:

There are actually two versions of Noah—Noah Pro, which costs $20, and Noah Lite, which is free. The difference? Noah Lite has a 37,000-word dictionary, while the Pro version comes with 122,000 words. You can also save memory in your Palm by storing the dictionary files for Noah Pro on a memory card; with Noah Lite, it all sits on your PDA. If you can live with those compromises, this is a must-have tool for getting through the day at work or school.

There are two ways to use Noah:

- Open the program and start entering a word. The dictionary immediately scrolls to the proper location as you enter characters, so entering "pen" will show a list of words that start with pen and then all the words that follow it in the dictionary. When you see the word you want, tap on it.

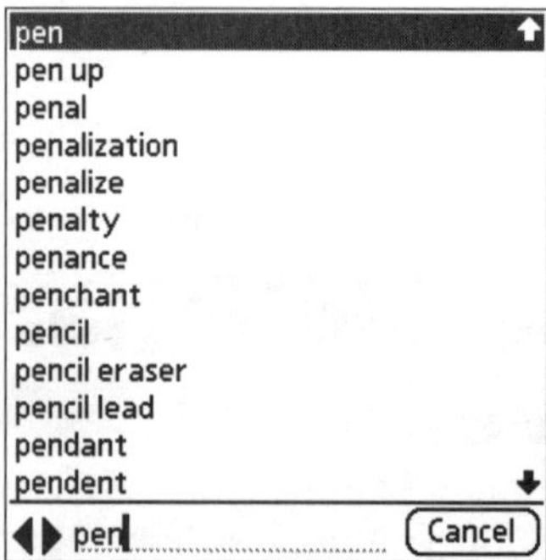

- If you see a word elsewhere on your Palm (such as in an e-book) that you don't understand, select the word and copy it to the clipboard by choosing Edit | Copy from the menu. Next, open Noah and tap the search icon on the right side of the screen (it's shaped like a magnifying glass). Then paste in the word from the clipboard—you can do this by making the Command gesture (a diagonal slash from the lower left to upper right of the Graffiti area) and tap the paste icon. Noah will automatically display the definition of that word if it's in the dictionary.

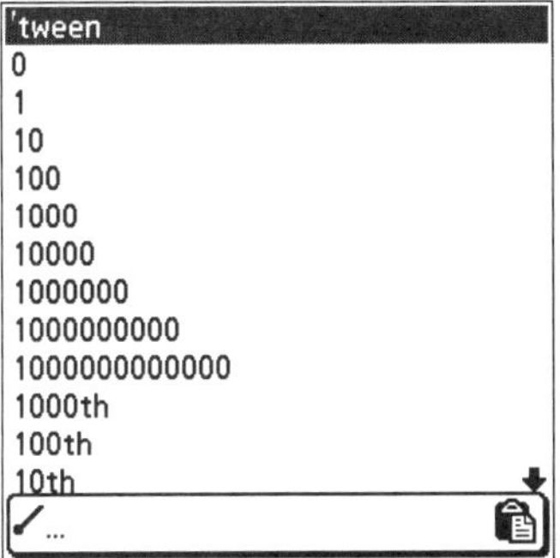

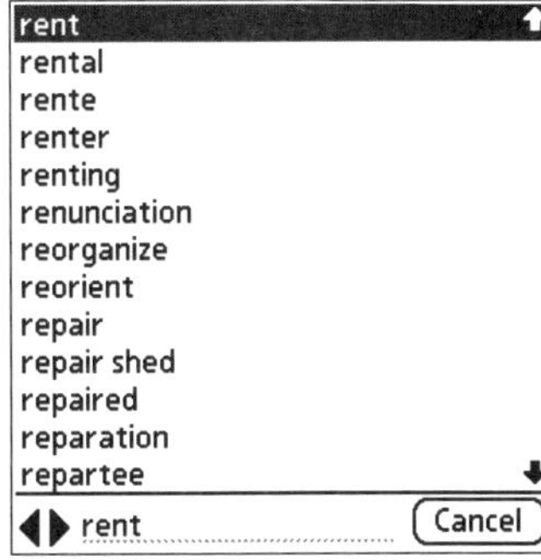

FIND IT ON THE CD
Noah Lite, Free
arsLexis
www.arslexis.com

100 Graffiti Anywhere

Write Anywhere

Having to write only in that tiny Graffiti area at the bottom of the screen is like being a dog that has to live in the hall closet. You get used to it after a while, but it's certainly not the way you'd envisioned your life.

If you want to break out of the tiny Graffiti area and write anywhere on the screen, you have a few choices. You could upgrade to a brand spanking new PDA that runs Graffiti 2, for instance, or you could pop a copy of Graffiti Anywhere onto your Palm.

Using the program is a snap. Just launch Graffiti Anywhere and tap the Enable button.

There are a bunch of options you can configure to taste, of course, and they're easy to explore. Tap the Activation tab, though, for the most important control. Here is where you determine when your Palm looks for Graffiti Anywhere on the screen. After all, if it accepted everything you input with the stylus as Graffiti, you'd never be able to tap buttons. By default, you need to press and hold the first button on your device. As long as you hold down the button, you can write on the screen. Release the button, and the Palm returns to normal.

Finally, notice that you get an "echo" when you use Graffiti Anywhere—by seeing what you write on the screen, you can actually get better at Graffiti and improve your accuracy.

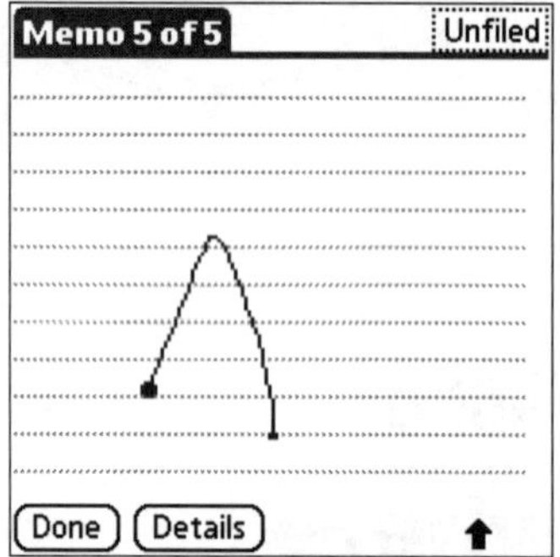

FIND IT ON THE CD

Graffiti Anywhere, Free
Thierry Escande
www.palmgear.com

Fab Foto Viewer

Some of the newer Palm OS PDAs come with image viewers built right in. If yours doesn't, you're missing out on the fun. Picture this: You have just taken a bunch of photos with your digital camera, and someone asks to see them. You can't really show off the images on the camera's LCD display—it's just too small. But you pop the SD Card out of the camera and place it in your PDA, then show off the images on the much larger PDA display. Problem solved! You might even want to simply use a PDA as a sort of digital wallet, showing off wallet-sized images that you've copied to your Palm's SD Card.

A program called JPEGView is just what you're looking for. This free utility can read images off of your SD Card and, well, display them. It doesn't do a lot, but it does get the job done.

To use JPEGView, just insert an SD Card with JPEG images into your PDA. Launch JPEGView and choose Document | Open Image from the menu. Navigate to the folder that holds your pictures and tap on one. Choose Open and wait while the picture is loaded into memory. To open another picture, just return to the menu and choose Open Image again.

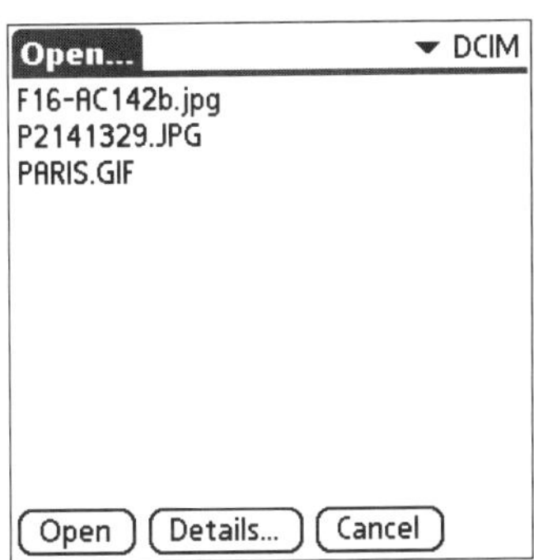

Killer Tip *Most digital cameras store their images in a folder called DCIM—so if you see a folder like that, tap on it and you'll find your pictures.*

JPEGView, Free
Margin Software
www.palmgear.com

Appendix

About the CD

The CD that comes with *101 Killer Apps for Your Palm Handheld* contains:

- Trial versions or shareware of a selection of the tools discussed in the book for you to try out
- Live links to the web sites where you can access the latest versions of all 101 Killer Apps covered in the book

We have included applications for download from those manufacturers who provided us with a written, signed agreement to include their applications on the CD. The applications discussed in the book—from 1 to 101—are all listed with their corresponding links to the latest version of each tool. Please note that the link on the CD was the latest version at the time the book and CD went to press.

Any tool listed on the CD that has a CD icon in the far left-hand column next to the tool name is available for download directly from the CD. Many of these tools are trial or demo versions that time-out after a certain period. For the latest version of the applications discussed in the book, you can use the URL next to each of the tools listed on the CD to access the manufacturers' web sites.

How to Use the CD-ROM

After you launch the CD, you will need to agree to the terms in the End User License Agreement. Once you agree, you will see the GNU Public License. After reading this, click the OK button. Clicking the authors' names will take you to a page with more information about the lead authors.

In the center of the cover there is a Link To 101 Apps button that will take you to the applications on the CD and to the links to all 101 Killer Apps discussed in the book. To the left of the cover, you will find bookmarks, which you can use to navigate to the different components on the CD. There, you will find information on how to use the CD and Adobe Acrobat Reader.

Applications on the CD

The Link To 101 Apps page includes all 101 Killer Apps discussed in the book, along with the latest URL for each tool, in case you need more information on how to install the tool or you want to download the most recent version online. When you click the application name, you may see a dialog that reads:

> "The file D:\OPENE~14.EXE is set to be launched by this PDF file. The file may contain programs, macros, or viruses that could potentially harm your computer. Only open the file if you are sure it is safe. If this file was placed by a trusted person or program then click Open to view this file."

Click the box that reads Do Not Show This Message Again, and click the Open button. Then, Acrobat will take you to the folder where all of the tools are located. There you will find folders for each of the tools. Double-click the tool you want to access, and then you will see the actual tool file ready for you to install on your system.

The table that follows lists the 101 Killer Apps included in the book. Applications with a CD icon are included on the CD.

NOTE *The links contained on the CD are the latest links available at the time the book went to press.*

	Killer App	Price	Company	URL
	1. Presenter-to-Go	$199	MARGI Systems	www.margi.com
	2. Thought-Manager	$39.95	Hands High Software	www.handshigh.com
CD	3. TAKEphONE	$19.95	ShSh	www.shsh.com
	4. MegaCalc	$14.95	MegaSoft-2000	www.megasoft2000.com
	5. Quickoffice	$39.95	iGo	www.quickoffice.com
CD	6. MobileDB	$19.95	Handmark	www.handmark.com
CD	7. ExpensePlus	$49.95	WalletWare	www.walletware.com
CD	8. RepliGo	$29.95	Cerience	www.cerience.com
CD	9. Documents To Go	$29.95	DataViz	www.dataviz.com
	10. Vindigo	$24.95 annual subscription	Vindigo	www.vindigo.com
CD	11. HandMap	$16 plus maps	HandMap	www.handmap.net
CD	12. Zagat To Go 2004	$24.95 (CD or download, one-year subscription)	Zagat	www.zagat.com
CD	13. English-French Talking Phrasebook	$19.95 (same price for other languages)	Beiks	www.beiks.com
CD	14. Small Talk	$19.95	LandWare	www.landware.com
CD	15. Gulliver	$19.99	Handmark	www.handmark.com
	16. Mapopolis Navigator	Free (maps extra)	Mapopolis	www.mapopolis.com

	Killer App	Price	Company	URL
	17. Palm Reader	Free	Palm Digital Media	www.palmdigitalmedia.com
	18. Wine Enthusiast Guide	$19.95	LandWare	www.landware.com
	19. BarBack Drink Guide	$9.95	Town Compass	www.pocketdirectory.com
	20. Movie-Mentor	$11.95 per year	Movie Mentor	www.moviementor.com
	21. Kinoma	$29.95	Kinoma	www.kinoma.com
	22. BalanceLog	$46	Healthe-Tech	www.healthetech.com
	23. Star Pilot Plus	$19.95	Star Pilot Tech-nologies	www.star-pilot.com
	24. TealAuto	$16.95	TealPoint	www.tealpoint.com
	25. SplashPhoto	$29.95	SplashData	www.splashdata.com
	26. AeroPlayer	$14.95	Aerodrome Software	www.aerodrome.us
	27. Pocket Cook Deluxe	$19.95	The Electronic Frontier, Ltd.	www.pocket-cook.com
	28. TealPaint	$17.95	TealPoint Software	www.tealpoint.com
	29. PalmMagic	$5	Ken Duncan	www.palmgear.com
	30. Audible.com	Free (but content available on subscription basis)	Audible	www.audible.com
	31. IntelliGolf 7.0 Birdie Edition	$39.95	Karrier Communications	www.intelligolf.com
	32. SimCity	$29.95	Atelier Software	www.ateliersoftware.com
	33. Merriam-Webster Crossword Challenge	$14.95	Hexacto	www.hexacto.com
	34. The Emperor's Mahjong	$14.95	Hexacto	www.hexacto.com
	35. Trivial Pursuit	$29.99	Handmark	www.handmark.com

	Killer App	Price	Company	URL
	36. Battleship, Scrabble, and Yahtzee	Battleship, $19.99 Scrabble, $29.99 Yahtzee, $19.99	Handmark	www.handmark.com
	37. All Mobile Casino	$17	Stand Alone	www.standalone.com
	38. ChessGenius	$25	Lang Software	www.chessgenius .com
	39. Backgammon Pro	$15	Stand Alone	www.standalone.com
	40. Billiards	$22.95	Megasoft2000	www.megasoft2000 .com
	41. Text Twist	$14.95	Astraware	www.astraware.com
	42. Aggression	$17.95	Blit Games	www.blitgames.com
	43. PDA Playground	$19.95	DataViz	www.dataviz.com
	44. Contacts 5	$19.95	PDA Performance	www.pdaperfor mance.com
	45. Agendus	$24.95	iambic	www.iambic.com
	46. ToDo PLUS	$19.95	Hands High Software	www.handshigh.com
	47. Memo PLUS	$19.95	Hands High Software	www.handshigh.com
	48. simpliWrite	$19.95	Advanced Recognition Technologies	www.simpliwrite .com
	49. MiddleCaps	Free	Rui Oliveria	www.palmgear.com
	50. Keyboard Hack II	$8.95	PalmGadget	www.palmgadget .com
	51. TapPad	$19.95	Brochu Software	www.tappad.com
	52. PenJammer	$9.90	Ironwheel Works	www.penjammer .com
	53. DualDate	Free	PalmOne	www.palmone.com
	54. Word-Complete	$24.99	Communication Intelligence Corporation	www.cic.com
	55. SilverScreen	$19.95	PocketSensei	www.pocketsensei .com

	Killer App	Price	Company	URL
	56. LearnFlash	$8	Bart Pinto	http://learnflash.virtualave.net
	57. WordSleuth Thesaurus	$14.95	LandWare	www.landware.com
	58. 4.0Student	$19.99	Handmark	www.handmark.com
	59. ePocrates Rx	Free	ePocrates, Inc.	www.epocrates.com
	60. The 2004 World Almanac, Handheld Edition Bundle	$11.95	Town Compass	www.pocket-directory.com
	61. Quizzler	Free	Pocket Mobility	www.pocketmobility.com
	62. Alphabet Rhyme Time	$5	Robert Jen	www.rjen.com
	63. PocketLingo Pro	$19.95	HLCSoft	www.pocketlingo.com
	64. Ultrasoft Money	$34.95	Ultrasoft	www.ultrasoft.com
	65. Pocket Quicken	$39.95	LandWare	www.landware.com
	66. Rebate Tracker	$8.99	XiY Technologies	www.xiy.net
	67. Stock Manager	$24.95	TinyStocks	www.tinystocks.com
	68. Money Magazine Financial Assistant	$19.95	LandWare	www.landware.com
	69. JackFlash	$19.95	Brayder Technologies, Inc.	www.brayder.com
	70. UnDupe	$7.95	Stevens Creek Software	www.stevenscreek.com
	71. 1 Button Pro	$20.00	Evans Software	www.palmgear.com
	72. Version-Tracker	Free	Versiontracker.com	www.versiontracker.com

Killer App	Price	Company	URL
73. NotSync	$9.95	UltraSoft	www.ultrasoft.com
74. PrintBoy	$39.95	Bachmann Software & Services	www.bachmannsoftware.com
75. Cloak	$19.95	Chapura	www.chapura.com
76. PDASecure Standard	$39.95	Trust Digital	www.trustdigital.com
77. AvantGo	Free	iAnywhere Solutions	www.avantgo.com
78. Room Builder	$14.95	Stand Alone, Inc.	www.standalone.com
79. AirClock	$19.95	AirSpell	www.airspell.com
80. StopWatch Pro	$9.95	Fresh Perspective Software	www.fps.com
81. BugMe	$19.95	Electric Pocket	www.electricpocket.com
82. Formulas for Palm OS	$12	Stand Alone, Inc.	www.standalone.com
83. DateMate	$19.95	MobiMate	www.mobimate.com
84. riteMail	$21.95	Pen&Internet	www.ritemail.net
85. HoliDates	$9.95	The Ripple Factory	www.theripplefactory.com
86. AOL for Palm OS	$19.95	America Online	http://anywhere.aol.com/pda
87. Freeware Pack	Free	PDAsoftnet	www.pdasoftnet.com/freepack
88. StreamLync 2.0	Free	PalmGear.com	www.palmgear.com
89. BigClock	Free	Jens Rupp	www.palmgear.com
90. Vexed	Free	James McCombe and the Vexed Team	http://vexed.sourceforge.net
91. Patience Revisited	Free	Paul Close	www.palmgear.com

Killer App	Price	Company	URL
92. Pocket Blackjack and Video Poker	Free	GoldPalm Casino, Inc.	www.palmgear.com
93. HandyShopper	Free	Christopher Antos	www.palmgear.com
94. DiddleBug	Free	Peter Putzer	www.palmgear.com
95. HappyDays	Free	Jaemok Jeong	www.palmgear.com
96. FileZ	Free	Nosleep Software	www.palmgear.com
97. Sketcher	Free	Palmetto Logic	www.palmgear.com
98. Loan Helper	Free	CobraPit	www.cobrapit.net/LoanHelper
99. Noah Lite	Free	arsLexis	www.arslexis.com
100. Graffiti Anywhere	Free	Thierry Escande	www.palmgear.com
101. JPEGView	Free	Margin Software	www.palmgear.com

Getting Started

The CD-ROM is optimized to run under Windows 95/98/NT/ME/2000/2003/XP/Server 2003 using the Adobe Acrobat Reader version 5.0 included on the disc. To install the tools on your computer, insert the CD into your CD disc drive. In most cases, a setup program will start automatically. (It may take a few moments for the opening windows to appear on your screen. If the indicator light is flashing on your CD drive, the program is still loading.)

Windows 95/98/NT/ME/2000/2003/XP/Server 2003

The CD will start automatically when you insert the CD in the drive. If the program does not start automatically, your system may not be set up to automatically detect CDs. You can start the program by double-clicking the My Computer icon on the Windows desktop. When the My Computer window opens, double-click the icon for your CD drive. The program should start. If it doesn't, you should now see a list of the CD's contents. Look for the file named start or start.exe. Double-click this file to start the program.

If you prefer, you can run the contents of the CD from your hard drive without having to use the CD. To do so, right-click the CD drive, select Open, copy the book folder to your hard drive, and install the version of Adobe Acrobat Reader supported by your operating system (see the instructions below). Once this is done, you can start the program by opening the book folder and double-clicking the file named cover or cover.pdf. This will automatically start the associated Acrobat Reader. For convenience, you can create a shortcut to the cover file and place it on your desktop. You will then be able to start the program by clicking the shortcut.

To install Acrobat Reader, double-click the My Computer icon on your desktop. When the My Computer window opens, double-click the icon for your CD drive. You should now see a list of the contents of the CD. Double-click the folder named Install. Within this folder, double-click the subfolder that corresponds to your version of the Windows operating system. In this folder, you will see a file named ar505enu or ar505enu.exe. Double-click this file to start the installation program. Alternatively, the most up-to-date version of Adobe Acrobat Reader is available for free download at www.adobe.com.

Windows 3.1

For Windows 3.1 users, you must use Acrobat Reader version 3.0, which is included on the CD. You must install the program on your hard drive. To install it, copy the book folder to your hard drive, and then install Acrobat Reader 3.0 for Windows. Then, to run the program, open the book folder and double-click the cover.pdf file.

Macintosh

For the CD to start automatically, you must be running under Mac OS version 8.6–9 (Autorun is not supported on Macintosh OS X). The title page should automatically display within a minute of inserting the CD. If the CD does not launch, you can start the program manually by double-clicking the CD-ROM icon on your desktop and then double-clicking the Start icon.

If you prefer, you can run the program from your hard drive without having to use the CD. To do so, copy the files to your hard drive and install Acrobat Reader.

Note *You must do this if you are using a 68K Macintosh.*

Unix

Go to www.adobe.com to locate Adobe Acrobat Reader for the following operating systems:

- Linux
- IBM AIX
- Sun OS
- SGI IRIX
- Sun Solaris
- HP-UX
- DEC OSF/1

To install the program, copy the book directory to your hard drive. Then install the appropriate version of Adobe Acrobat Reader. You may then start the program from your hard drive.

Problems with the CD

If you have followed the instructions above, and the program will not work, you may have a defective drive or a defective CD. Be sure the CD is inserted properly in the drive. (Test the drive with other CDs to see if they run.)

If you live in the U.S. and the CD included in your book has defects in materials or workmanship, please call McGraw-Hill at 1-800-217-0059, 9 A.M. to 5 P.M. (EST), Monday through Friday, and McGraw-Hill will replace the defective disc. If you live outside the U.S., please contact your local McGraw-Hill office. You can find contact information for most offices on the International Contact Information page immediately following the index of this book, or send an e-mail to omg_international@mcgraw-hill.com.

Index

Numbers

A

B

C

D

E

F

G

H

U

V

W

X

Y

Z

INTERNATIONAL CONTACT INFORMATION

AUSTRALIA
McGraw-Hill Book Company
Australia Pty. Ltd.
TEL +61-2-9900-1800
FAX +61-2-9878-8881
http://www.mcgraw-hill.com.au
books-it_sydney@mcgraw-hill.com

CANADA
McGraw-Hill Ryerson Ltd.
TEL +905-430-5000
FAX +905-430-5020
http://www.mcgraw-hill.ca

GREECE, MIDDLE EAST, & AFRICA (Excluding South Africa)
McGraw-Hill Hellas
TEL +30-210-6560-990
TEL +30-210-6560-993
TEL +30-210-6560-994
FAX +30-210-6545-525

MEXICO (Also serving Latin America)
McGraw-Hill Interamericana Editores
S.A. de C.V.
TEL +525-1500-5108
FAX +525-117-1589
http://www.mcgraw-hill.com.mx
carlos_ruiz@mcgraw-hill.com

SINGAPORE (Serving Asia)
McGraw-Hill Book Company
TEL +65-6863-1580
FAX +65-6862-3354
http://www.mcgraw-hill.com.sg
mghasia@mcgraw-hill.com

SOUTH AFRICA
McGraw-Hill South Africa
TEL +27-11-622-7512
FAX +27-11-622-9045
robyn_swanepoel@mcgraw-hill.com

SPAIN
McGraw-Hill/
Interamericana de España, S.A.U.
TEL +34-91-180-3000
FAX +34-91-372-8513
http://www.mcgraw-hill.es
professional@mcgraw-hill.es

UNITED KINGDOM, NORTHERN, EASTERN, & CENTRAL EUROPE
McGraw-Hill Education Europe
TEL +44-1-628-502500
FAX +44-1-628-770224
http://www.mcgraw-hill.co.uk
emea_queries@mcgraw-hill.com

ALL OTHER INQUIRIES Contact:
McGraw-Hill/Osborne
TEL +1-510-420-7700
FAX +1-510-420-7703
http://www.osborne.com
omg_international@mcgraw-hill.com

The GNU License

Linux is written and distributed under the GNU General Public License which means that its source code is freely-distributed and available to the general public.

GNU GENERAL PUBLIC LICENSE
Version 2, June 1991

Preamble

The licenses for most software are designed to take away your freedom to share and change it. By contrast, the GNU General Public License is intended to guarantee your freedom to share and change free software—to make sure the software is free for all its users. This General Public License applies to most of the Free Software Foundation's software and to any other program whose authors commit to using it. (Some other Free Software Foundation software is covered by the GNU Library General Public License instead.) You can apply it to your programs, too.

When we speak of free software, we are referring to freedom, not price. Our General Public Licenses are designed to make sure that you have the freedom to distribute copies of free software (and charge for this service if you wish), that you receive source code or can get it if you want it, that you can change the software or use pieces of it in new free programs; and that you know you can do these things.

To protect your rights, we need to make restrictions that forbid anyone to deny you these rights or to ask you to surrender the rights. These restrictions translate to certain responsibilities for you if you distribute copies of the software, or if you modify it.

For example, if you distribute copies of such a program, whether gratis or for a fee, you must give the recipients all the rights that you have. You must make sure that they, too, receive or can get the source code. And you must show them these terms so they know their rights.

We protect your rights with two steps: (1) copyright the software, and (2) offer you this license which gives you legal permission to copy, distribute and/or modify the software.

Also, for each author's protection and ours, we want to make certain that everyone understands that there is no warranty for this free software. If the software is modified by someone else and passed on, we want its recipients to know that what they have is not the original, so that any problems introduced by others will not reflect on the original authors' reputations.

Finally, any free program is threatened constantly by software patents. We wish to avoid the danger that redistributors of a free program will individually obtain patent licenses, in effect making the program proprietary. To prevent this, we have made it clear that any patent must be licensed for everyone's free use or not licensed at all.

The precise terms and conditions for copying, distribution and modification follow.

GNU GENERAL PUBLIC LICENSE TERMS AND CONDITIONS FOR COPYING,
DISTRIBUTION AND MODIFICATION

0. This License applies to any program or other work which contains a notice placed by the copyright holder saying it may be distributed under the terms of this General Public License. The "Program", below, refers to any such program or work, and a "work based on the Program" means either the Program or any derivative work under copyright law: that is to say, a work containing the Program or a portion of it, either verbatim or with modifications and/or translated into another language. (Hereinafter, translation is included without limitation in the term "modification".) Each licensee is addressed as "you".

Activities other than copying, distribution and modification are not covered by this License; they are outside its scope. The act of running the Program is not restricted, and the output from the Program is covered only if its contents constitute a work based on the Program (independent of having been made by running the Program). Whether that is true depends on what the Program does.

1. You may copy and distribute verbatim copies of the Program's source code as you receive it, in any medium, provided that you conspicuously and appropriately publish on each copy an appropriate copyright notice and disclaimer of warranty; keep intact all the notices that refer to this License and to the absence of any warranty; and give any other recipients of the Program a copy of this License along with the Program.

You may charge a fee for the physical act of transferring a copy, and you may at your option offer warranty protection in exchange for a fee.

2. You may modify your copy or copies of the Program or any portion of it, thus forming a work based on the Program, and copy and distribute such modifications or work under the terms of Section 1 above, provided that you also meet all of these conditions:

a) You must cause the modified files to carry prominent notices stating that you changed the files and the date of any change.

b) You must cause any work that you distribute or publish, that in whole or in part contains or is derived from the Program or any part thereof, to be licensed as a whole at no charge to all third parties under the terms of this License.

c) If the modified program normally reads commands interactively when run, you must cause it, when started running for such interactive use in the most ordinary way, to sprint or display an announcement including an appropriate copyright notice and a notice that there is no warranty (or else, saying that you provide a warranty) and that users may redistribute the program under these conditions, and telling the user how to view a copy of this License. (Exception: if the Program itself is interactive but does not normally print such an announcement, your work based on the Program is not required to print an announcement.)

These requirements apply to the modified work as a whole. If identifiable sections of that work are not derived from the Program, and can be reasonably considered independent and separate works in themselves, then this License, and its terms, do not apply to those sections when you distribute them as separate works. But when you distribute the same sections as part of a whole which is a work based on the Program, the distribution of the whole must be on the terms of this License, whose permissions for other licensees extend to the entire whole, and thus to each and every part regardless of who wrote it. Thus, it is not the intent of this section to claim rights or contest your rights to work written entirely by you; rather, the intent is to exercise the right to control the distribution of derivative or collective works based on the Program.

In addition, mere aggregation of another work not based on the Program with the Program (or with a work based on the Program) on a volume of a storage or distribution medium does not bring the other work under the scope of this License.

3. You may copy and distribute the Program (or a work based on it, under Section 2) in object code or executable form under the terms of Sections 1 and 2 above provided that you also do one of the following:

a) Accompany it with the complete corresponding machine-readable source code, which must be distributed under the terms of Sections 1 and 2 above on a medium customarily used for software interchange; or,

b) Accompany it with a written offer, valid for at least three years, to give any third party, for a charge no more than your cost of physically performing source distribution, a complete machine-readable copy of the corresponding source code, to be distributed under the terms of Sections 1 and 2 above on a medium customarily used for software interchange; or,

c) Accompany it with the information you received as to the offer to distribute corresponding source code. (This alternative is allowed only for noncommercial distribution and only if you received the program in object code or executable form with such an offer, in accord with Subsection b above.)

The source code for a work means the preferred form of the work for making modifications to it. For an executable work, complete source code means all the source code for all modules it contains, plus any associated interface definition files, plus the scripts used to control compilation and installation of the executable. However, as a special exception, the source code distributed need not include anything that is normally distributed (in either source or binary form) with the major components (compiler, kernel, and so on) of the operating system on which the executable runs, unless that component itself accompanies the executable.

If distribution of executable or object code is made by offering access to copy from a designated place, then offering equivalent access to copy the source code from the same place counts as distribution of the source code, even though third parties are not compelled to copy the source along with the object code.

4. You may not copy, modify, sublicense, or distribute the Program except as expressly provided under this License. Any attempt otherwise to copy, modify, sublicense or distribute the Program is void, and will automatically terminate your rights under this License. However, parties who have received copies, or rights, from you under this License will not have their licenses terminated so long as such parties remain in full compliance.

5. You are not required to accept this License, since you have not signed it. However, nothing else grants you permission to modify or distribute the Program or its derivative works. These actions are prohibited by law if you do not accept this License. Therefore, by modifying or distributing the Program (or any work based on the Program), you indicate your acceptance of this License to do so, and all its terms and conditions for copying, distributing or modifying the Program or works based on it.

6. Each time you redistribute the Program (or any work based on the Program), the recipient automatically receives a license from the original licensor to copy, distribute or modify the Program subject to these terms and conditions. You may not impose any further restrictions on the recipients' exercise of the rights granted herein. You are not responsible for enforcing compliance by third parties to this License.

7. If, as a consequence of a court judgment or allegation of patent infringement or for any other reason (not limited to patent issues), conditions are imposed on you (whether by court order, agreement or otherwise) that contradict the conditions of this License, they do not excuse you from the conditions of this License. If you cannot distribute so as to satisfy simultaneously your obligations under this License and any other pertinent obligations, then as a consequence you may not distribute the Program at all. For example, if a patent license would not permit royalty-free redistribution of the Program by all those who receive copies directly or indirectly through you, then the only way you could satisfy both it and this License would be to refrain entirely from distribution of the Program.

If any portion of this section is held invalid or unenforceable under any particular circumstance, the balance of the section is intended to apply and the section as a whole is intended to apply in other circumstances.

It is not the purpose of this section to induce you to infringe any patents or other property right claims or to contest validity of any such claims; this section has the sole purpose of protecting the integrity of the free software distribution system, which is implemented by public license practices. Many people have made generous contributions to the wide range of software distributed through that system in reliance on consistent application of that system; it is up to the author/donor to decide if he or she is willing to distribute software through any other system and a licensee cannot impose that choice.

This section is intended to make thoroughly clear what is believed to be a consequence of the rest of this License.

8. If the distribution and/or use of the Program is restricted in certain countries either by patents or by copyrighted interfaces, the original copyright holder who places the Program under this License may add an explicit geographical distribution limitation excluding those countries, so that distribution is permitted only in or among countries not thus excluded. In such case, this License incorporates the limitation as if written in the body of this License.

9. The Free Software Foundation may publish revised and/or new versions of the General Public License from time to time. Such new versions will be similar in spirit to the present version, but may differ in detail to address new problems or concerns.

Each version is given a distinguishing version number. If the Program specifies a version number of this License which applies to it and "any later version", you have the option of following the terms and conditions either of that version or of any later version published by the Free Software Foundation. If the Program does not specify a version number of this License, you may choose any version ever published by the Free Software Foundation.

10. If you wish to incorporate parts of the Program into other free programs whose distribution conditions are different, write to the author to ask for permission. For software which is copyrighted by the Free Software Foundation, write to the Free Software Foundation;

we sometimes make exceptions for this. Our decision will be guided by the two goals of preserving the free status of all derivatives of our free software and of promoting the sharing and reuse of software generally.

NO WARRANTY

11. BECAUSE THE PROGRAM IS LICENSED FREE OF CHARGE, THERE IS NO WARRANTY FOR THE PROGRAM, TO THE EXTENT PERMITTED BY APPLICABLE LAW. EXCEPT WHEN OTHERWISE STATED IN WRITING THE COPYRIGHT HOLDERS AND/OR OTHER PARTIES PROVIDE THE PROGRAM "AS IS" WITHOUT WARRANTY OF ANY KIND, EITHER EXPRESSED OR IMPLIED, INCLUDING, BUT NOT LIMITED TO, THE IMPLIED WARRANTIES OF MERCHANTABILITY AND FITNESS FOR A PARTICULAR PURPOSE. THE ENTIRE RISK AS TO THE QUALITY AND PERFORMANCE OF THE PROGRAM IS WITH YOU. SHOULD THE PROGRAM PROVE DEFECTIVE, YOU ASSUME THE COST OF ALL NECESSARY SERVICING, REPAIR OR CORRECTION.

12. IN NO EVENT UNLESS REQUIRED BY APPLICABLE LAW OR AGREED TO IN WRITING WILL ANY COPYRIGHT HOLDER, OR ANY OTHER PARTY WHO MAY MODIFY AND/OR REDISTRIBUTE THE PROGRAM AS PERMITTED ABOVE, BE LIABLE TO YOU FOR DAMAGES, INCLUDING ANY GENERAL, SPECIAL, INCIDENTAL OR CONSEQUENTIAL DAMAGES ARISING OUT OF THE USE OR INABILITY TO USE THE PROGRAM (INCLUDING BUT NOT LIMITED TO LOSS OF DATA OR DATA BEING RENDERED INACCURATE OR LOSSES SUSTAINED BY YOU OR THIRD PARTIES OR A FAILURE OF THE PROGRAM TO OPERATE WITH ANY OTHER PROGRAMS), EVEN IF SUCH HOLDER OR OTHER PARTY HAS BEEN ADVISED OF THE POSSIBILITY OF SUCH DAMAGES.

END OF TERMS AND CONDITIONS

Appendix: How to Apply These Terms to Your New Programs

If you develop a new program, and you want it to be of the greatest possible use to the public, the best way to achieve this is to make it free software which everyone can redistribute and change under these terms.

To do so, attach the following notices to the program. It is safest to attach them to the start of each source file to most effectively convey the exclusion of warranty; and each file should have at least the "copyright" line and a pointer to where the full notice is found.

> <one line to give the program's name and a brief idea of what it does.> Copyright (C) 19yy <name of author>
>
> This program is free software; you can redistribute it and/or modify it under the terms of the GNU General Public License as published by the Free Software Foundation; either version 2 of the License, or (at your option) any later version.
>
> This program is distributed in the hope that it will be useful, but WITHOUT ANY WARRANTY; without even the implied warranty of MERCHANTABILITY or FITNESS FOR A PARTICULAR PURPOSE. See the GNU General Public License for more details.
>
> You should have received a copy of the GNU General Public License along with this program; if not, write to the Free Software Foundation, Inc., 675 Mass Ave, Cambridge, MA 02139, USA.

Also add information on how to contact you by electronic and paper mail.

If the program is interactive, make it output a short notice like this when it starts in an interactive mode:

> Gnomovision version 69, Copyright (C) 19yy name of author Gnomovision comes with ABSOLUTELY NO WARRANTY; for details type `show w'. This is free software, and you are welcome to redistribute it under certain conditions; type `show c' for details.

The hypothetical commands `show w' and `show c' should show the appropriate parts of the General Public License. Of course, the commands you use may be called something other than `show w' and `show c'; they could even be mouse-clicks or menu items—whatever suits your program.

You should also get your employer (if you work as a programmer) or your school, if any, to sign a "copyright disclaimer" for the program, if necessary. Here is a sample; alter the names:

> Yoyodyne, Inc., hereby disclaims all copyright interest in the program `Gnomovision' (which makes passes at compilers) written by James Hacker.
>
> <signature of Ty Coon>, 1 April 1989
> Ty Coon, President of Vice

This General Public License does not permit incorporating your program into proprietary programs. If your program is a subroutine library, you may consider it more useful to permit linking proprietary applications with the library. If this is what you want to do, use the GNU Library General Public License instead of this License.